The Chicken Soup Book

The Chicken Soup Book

OLD AND NEW RECIPES FROM AROUND THE WORLD

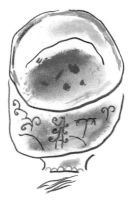

BY JANET HAZEN

ILLUSTRATIONS BY LILLA ROGERS

CHRONICLE BOOKS

SAN FRANCISCO

Library of Congress Cataloging-in-Publication Data:

Hazen, Janet.
    The chicken soup book: old and new recipes from around
the world / by Janet Hazen ; illustrations by Lilla Rogers.
        p.   cm.
    Includes index.
    ISBN 0-8118-0461-5
    1. Soups.   2. Cookery (Chicken).   3. Cookery, International.
I. Title.
TX757.H37 1994
641.8 ' 13—dc20   93-39580
                                                              CIP

Printed in Hong Kong.

Distributed in Canada by Raincoast Books,
112 East Third Avenue, Vancouver, B.C. V5T 1C8

10 9 8 7 6 5 4 3 2 1

Chronicle Books
275 Fifth Street
San Francisco, CA 94103

*This book is dedicated
in loving memory to Jacob,
a presence and force that entered my life
over eighteen years ago.
At once a cohort and opponent,
a friend and lover, a source of pure joy
and, at times, complete frustration,
Jacob filled my life,
whether I was ready or not,
in a most complete and compelling way.
At last, Jacob, I present to you
an expanded version
of your own "Jewish penicillin."
Within the pages of this book
you may uncover a delectable potion
designed for eternal bliss and solace.
It is intended for you, my friend,
and for all those who seek everlasting peace.
Your spirit lives in my heart.*

Table of Contents

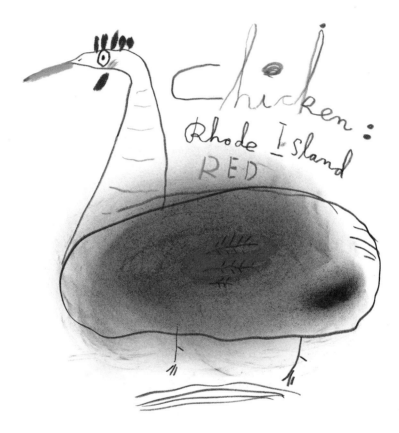

Chicken:
Rhode I Sland
RED

INTRODUCTION

As an antidote for colds and flu, depression, bad report cards, upset stomachs, cramps, political unrest, allergies, bronchitis, arthritis, and hangnails, a bowl of steaming hot chicken soup is cherished in most every part of the world. Whether it be a soup made from velvety strands of delicate white meat floating in a fragrant broth studded with fresh corn, asparagus, and a hint of soy sauce, or a hearty soup thick with plump chick-peas, black olives, chunks of tender dark meat, garlic, and rosemary, chicken soup is clearly a universal cure-all. If in fact "Jewish penicillin" doesn't *solve* life's most stubborn problems, it at least relieves many of the symptoms.

Each country and certainly every cuisine has at least one version of this restorative dish. When I began research on this book, I uncovered a plethora of soup recipes built around one essential ingredient—the ubiquitous chicken. Depending on the country, a myriad of compatible vegetables, grains, spices, herbs, flavoring agents, and in some cases, meat and seafood, are added to the pot. As a result, some recipes are complex and intricate, others simple and straightforward, but all are rewarding to make.

The Principles of Making Chicken Soup gives guidelines for buying, cooking, cutting, and storing chicken, as well as the fundamentals of making chicken stock. The Basic Recipes chapter provides two recipes for basic chicken stock which are used throughout the book. The Notes on Ingredients section at the end gives directions for roasting fresh chili and bell peppers, preparing and trimming fresh baby artichoke hearts, and cutting and washing fresh leeks.

The recipe portion of this book is divided into six chapters: North, Central, and South America; Asia and the South Pacific; Africa and the Caribbean; India and the Middle East; the Mediterranean; and Northern Europe, Russia, and the Adriatic. While it was difficult to limit the quantity of recipes and the number of countries, I feel that each region is fairly represented in this collection. As a result, this book is valuable not only as an important resource for chicken soup recipes, but also as a guide to ethnic cooking styles, techniques, and ingredients. For example, the chapter on Asian and South Pacific soups contains information about typical ingredients used in Thai, Vietnamese, Chinese, Filipino, and Indonesian cooking, as well as specific cuisines of the South Pacific, namely, Tahiti and Hawaii.

Most of the recipes in this book yield approximately ten to twelve cups of soup. All recipes can be halved, but I prefer making large batches of soup—after all, it takes almost the same time to prepare twelve cups of soup as it does to make only six cups. A large pot of soup can take a small family through several days of meals, or supply a large family with one or two satisfying meals. Since most of these soups can be frozen successfully, I urge you to make the full recipe, perhaps reserving half for weeknight meals and freezing the remainder to enjoy later. If stored in a tightly sealed container in the refrigerator, most soups will keep for up to five days. Recipes made with hearty root vegetables, beans, and grains are the best candidates for storing and reheating. Those made with cheese or finished with eggs are more deli-cate and must be reheated over a low flame, but virtually all of these soups can be reheated a second time successfully. When reheating soup, remove only the portion you intend to serve. Heat the soup in a small saucepan over moderate heat until warmed through. Do not reheat the entire batch of soup; repeated and unnecessary heating or rapid boiling can break down the ingredients and weaken the flavor.

When freezing soups, store the cooled soup in a plastic container with a tight-fitting lid, labeled with the kind of soup, perhaps the ingredients, and the date it was cooked. Remember, liquids expand when frozen, so leave about one inch of headroom between the top of the soup and the lid. Freeze soups no longer than four months for optimal taste and preservation of texture and color.

Nearly all of the recipes in this book call for chicken meat in one form or another. Both white and dark chicken are used, either coarsely chopped, shredded, or minced. When a recipe calls for precooked chicken it will specify "cooked" chicken; if it does not, use uncooked chicken. Since white chicken meat takes only a few minutes to cook, it is always added during the last five or ten minutes of cooking. If a recipe calls for uncooked white chicken meat, and you happen to have some cooked chicken meat around, by all means use it in the recipe by adding it during the last five to seven minutes of cooking. Since the meat is already cooked, it only needs to be thoroughly heated.

I hope you encounter the same kind of comfort and pleasure I enjoyed while testing this collection of chicken soup recipes. Many are international classics, revised and updated to improve their flavor and texture and to increase their visual appeal. Others are new creations that draw from the indigenous ingredients, cooking styles and techniques, and culinary customs of a given area. Eating chicken soup as a step toward health and prosperity is indeed an axiom, but don't use these stimulating, aromatic, irresistible soup recipes just for their curative effects; include them in your everyday diet and experience a world of multicultural cooking and eating.

The Principles of Making Chicken Soup

Purchasing Chicken: Virtually any size chicken can be used for making stock or chicken soup. Choose fresh poultry with smooth, unblemished skin wrapped tightly around plump flesh. Fresh chicken carries very little odor—if chicken gives off any kind of strong, rancid, or gamy smell, chances are it is past its prime and shouldn't be purchased.

Broilers generally weigh between 1½ and 2½ pounds, and fryers between 2½ and 3½ pounds; they can be of either gender, but both must be between 9 and 12 weeks old to qualify as a broiler or fryer. A roaster is a young chicken of either gender between the ages of 3 and 5 months. They can weigh anywhere from 3½ to 5 pounds each. Less common is the capon—a castrated male chicken under 8 months old, weighing between 5 and 8 pounds. Frequently sold as "stewing hen," this female bird is generally over 10 months of age, and weighs 3½ to 6 pounds. The younger the bird, the more tender the flesh. Conversely, older birds tend to have tougher meat, and often have a more assertive taste. All chickens, regardless of age, are suitable for using in stocks, but when chicken meat is needed, it's best to use a younger, smaller bird. For making recipes in this book, your safest best is a broiler, fryer, or roaster, since they are the most versatile and readily available.

I would strongly urge that you look for free-range or naturally-raised poultry as an alternative to commercially-raised chicken. These birds, along with their obvious health advantages, have a texture and flavor far superior to their chemical and hormone-infused relatives.

Storing Chicken: Cut-up poultry is more perishable than whole birds, but any poultry must be refrigerated until ready to use—regardless of size, shape, age, or type.

When buying chicken wrapped in airtight bags, remove the original wrapper and replace with a loose-fitting plastic bag or waxed paper before storing in your refrigerator. Chicken procured from the meat counter and immediately wrapped in white butcher paper can be stored in your refrigerator as is. Previously frozen and thawed chicken must not be frozen a second time, but fresh poultry can be tightly wrapped in two layers of foil or plastic and stored in the freezer for up to 4 months. It is best to use fresh chicken right away, but refrigerating it one or two days is also fine. Do not keep fresh chicken in your refrigerator longer than 3 days.

To defrost poultry, remove from the freezer and place it in a shallow pan in the refrigerator. Depending on the size, it will take 1 to 2 days to thoroughly thaw. Alternatively, place the frozen bird in a large bowl and cover with cold water for 4 to 6 hours. Change the water every hour or so, checking the chicken's texture each time. When the bird is pliable and supple, it is ready to cook. Thawed chicken must be cooked the same day.

Cooking Chicken: Since many of the recipes in this book call for cooked chicken meat, I find it convenient to add those pieces to the simmering stock, removing them when they are done. This way you have cooked chicken meat ready to use in the recipe, while adding even more flavor to the stock. For example, when a recipe calls for 2 cups of cooked-dark chicken meat, I add three or four thighs to the stock, and remove them when they are cooked through.

Generally speaking, dark chicken meat takes longer to cook than white meat. For this reason, it's difficult to cook chicken breasts and thighs together in the same pot for the same length of time with good results. However, if you wish to cook both white and dark pieces together, add them to the pot at the same time and remove them separately when each is cooked through. White meat pieces take approximately 20 minutes, dark meat pieces about 40 to 45 minutes.

To cook white meat when time is not an issue, I like to cook chicken breasts using a fail-safe Chinese method: Place the unboned chicken breasts in a large pot and cover with cold water. Bring to a boil over high heat and cook 5 minutes. Remove from the heat, cover with a tight-fitting lid, and let stand at room temperature for 2 to 2½ hours. Remove the chicken and separate the bones from the meat. Save the bones for stock or discard, and prepare the chicken meat according to the recipe.

When pressed for time, place the unboned chicken breasts in a large pot and cover with cold water. Bring to a boil over high heat, reduce the heat to moderate, and simmer approximately 20 minutes, or until the interior is opaque and the liquids run clear when the breast is pierced with a sharp knife. Remove the chicken from the water and drain in a colander. Boned and skinned chicken breasts take 5 to 7 minutes to cook; do not overcook the white meat or it will be tough, dry, and chewy.

To cook dark meat until very tender, follow the same directions as for cooking white chicken meat when pressed for time, but extend the cooking time to 1 hour or 1 hour and 15 minutes, depending on the size and quantity of chicken pieces.

Cutting Chicken Meat: Slicing and chopping cooked chicken is easy—all that is required is a sharp knife and a clean cutting board. To facilitate cutting and slicing uncooked chicken meat, wrap the meat in plastic and place in the freezer for about 30 minutes, or until it is firm to the touch. Slightly freezing the meat makes cutting much easier, especially when cutting into fine dice or mincing. When finished cutting chicken, *always scrub the cutting board with hot water and dish soap.*

What to do with Chicken Fat: In this time of heightened health consciousness, chicken fat might be considered taboo, but cooks of many cultures would think discarding it an unconscionable act. Like other saturated fats, a small amount goes a long way, and the marvelous flavor of good chicken fat is unsurpassed. I like to remove the fat from the surface of the stock and store it in a tightly covered plastic container or jar in the refrigerator. As long as the fat is free of bits of chicken or liquid, it can last several months in the refrigerator. I like to use the fat when making a roux for soups or sauces, for sauteing root vegetables, for adding to mashed potatoes, and for adding to cooked grains and beans. Some of the recipes in this book call for it when sauteing onions, garlic, and other vegetables for soup.

Stock Pot

celery   carrot   bay leaf

Making Basic Chicken Stock: The basic recipes for making chicken stock are given in the Basic Recipes chapter; however, there are a few fundamental guidelines to follow when preparing stock.

A chicken stock is a clear, water-based liquid flavored by the soluble substances extracted from chicken meat, bones, and cartilage and from vegetables, herbs, and spices. When preparing a chicken stock, it is important to use only the most wholesome ingredients; a stockpot is not the place to use up old, less-than-desirable produce or chicken that is past its prime. Blemished or misshapen produce is fine, but use only the freshest poultry meat and bones.

Never include chicken livers in stock because they can turn the stock bitter. Avoid celery leaves for the same reason. Onion skins can go into the stockpot, as well as unpeeled but washed carrots. This is the time to use those slightly wilted scallions and the (washed) outer leaves from leeks.

Bones are the major ingredient of stock, but when making a traditional chicken stock, several stalks of celery, a few carrots, an onion or two, parsley, a bay leaf and perhaps some whole black peppercorns are also added for extra flavor. For most purposes, a small amount of these vegetables is added to a basic chicken stock to round out the flavors and add body. If you want a pure, unadulterated chicken broth, however, it's best to use only poultry products and omit the vegetables. This kind of stock is ideal when making a reduction to use with poultry, fish, pork, or vegetables.

The best chicken stock is made from the bones of uncooked chicken plus a few pieces of chicken with meat remaining on the bones. When choosing chicken parts to include in stock, pick those with a higher percentage of bone to meat; wings, backs, and necks are suitable for using in stock. When making a chicken stock, you ultimately want a clear liquid packed with the essence of chicken, rather than a cloudy mixture that barely hints of poultry flavor.

When cooking stock, always begin with cold water to speed extraction—hot water delays extraction because in it many proteins are not soluble. Once the water comes to a boil, always remove the foamy scum from the surface. If it is not removed, the light brown scum, which is an accumulation of fat, coagulated protein, and impurities in the meat, will make the stock cloudy and could impart a bitter flavor. Do not let the stock boil as rapid cooking breaks up the solids into tiny particles that eventually make the stock cloudy. Keep the water level above the bones, and add more water as necessary when the stock reduces below this level.

Chicken stocks generally require three to four hours of cooking time in order to extract all the vital elements, gelatin, and flavor. Stocks cooked for shorter periods of time are weak and thin; conversely, over-cooked stocks can be bitter and cloudy.

Canned Chicken Broth versus Homemade Chicken Stock: High-quality canned chicken broth can be used as an alternative to homemade chicken stock in most instances. In cases where it is not interchangeable, for example in the Italian Chicken Broth with Potato Gnocchi, the recipe will specify homemade stock only. Most canned broths contain unwanted ingredients such as dextrose, MSG, yeast extracts, artificial coloring, and large amounts of sodium. For this reason, and because the liquid has little, if any, body, they are less desirable. Due to its high salt content, when boiled rapidly over an extended period of time, canned broth can become intensely salty, making it virtually inedible. Secondly, unlike homemade stock, canned chicken broth does not thicken as it cooks and therefore cannot be cooked down to a viscous sauce or reduction.

Natural food stores and some grocery stores carry broth made without MSG or sodium, and some popular brands produce a low-sodium chicken broth. If you must substitute canned chicken broth, try to use only those made with few, if any, additives, and/or those with a low sodium content. Always taste soups made with canned broth before adding additional salt.

BASIC RECIPES

Strong Chicken Stock

This chicken stock is made primarily with chicken bones and a few stock vegetables, and as a result the flavor is more direct than one made with chicken meat and a larger percent of vegetables. Use this stock when you want a soup base with concentrated chicken flavor and lots of body.

Ask your butcher for assorted chicken bones, or buy whole chickens (or cut-up chicken parts) and have him or her remove the meat from the bones for this stock. Save the meat to use in recipes that call for uncooked chicken meat. Cooked down to approximately 2 cups, the strained stock forms an intensely flavored "reduction," ideal for using as a sauce or glaze for poultry, fish, and pork or for potatoes, vegetables, pasta, or grains.

MAKES ABOUT 3 QUARTS.

Bones from 2 whole uncooked chickens (4 breasts, 4 thighs,
*   4 legs, 4 wings, 2 backs, and 2 necks)*
4 chicken wings
6 chicken feet (optional)
10 quarts cold water
1 large carrot, cut into 1-inch pieces
2 stalks celery, cut into 1-inch pieces
2 large onions, cut into eighths

Place the bones, wings, and feet in a 12-quart stockpot. Add 8 quarts of cold water. Bring to a boil over high heat. Using a large slotted spoon, skim the frothy foam from the surface and discard. Add the carrot, celery, and onions and return to the boil over high heat. Again remove the frothy foam from the surface and discard. Reduce the heat to moderate and simmer for 1½ hours, skimming the foam as it accumulates during the initial stage of cooking.

Add the remaining 2 quarts of cold water and return to the boil over high heat. Reduce the heat to moderate and simmer for 1½ to 2 hours. Remove from the heat and cool to room temperature. Skim the fat from the surface and discard, or save for cooking.

Strain the mixture through a colander set over a large pot or bowl. Discard the bones and vegetables. Transfer the strained stock to a nonreactive container with a tight-fitting lid. Store in the refrigerator for up to 5 days, or in the freezer for up to 4 months.

Light Chicken Stock

This recipe, which is made with chicken pieces, has a less intense chicken flavor than one made primarily with chicken bones. A greater ratio of traditional stock vegetables such as carrots, onions, and celery combined with whole black peppercorns and bay leaves gives this chicken stock a round and balanced flavor, ideal for soups that require, or benefit from, additional tones and layers of flavor.

This stock tends to be more cloudy than one made with bones, but the flavor is still wonderful.

MAKES ABOUT 4 ½ QUARTS.

6 chicken wings
20 chicken feet (or 3 chicken backs)
3 chicken legs
3 chicken thighs
10 quarts cold water
2 large carrots, cut into 1-inch pieces
4 stalks celery, cut into 1-inch pieces
2 large onions, cut into eighths
2 bay leaves
1 rounded tablespoon whole black peppercorns

Place the chicken wings, feet, legs, and thighs in a 12-quart stock pot. Add 8 quarts of cold water. Bring to a boil over high heat. Using a large slotted spoon, skim the frothy foam from the surface and discard. Reduce the heat to moderate and simmer for 1 hour, skimming the foam from the surface as it accumulates during the initial stage of cooking.

Add the carrots, celery, onions, bay leaves, and black peppercorns; return to the boil over high heat. Reduce the heat to moderate and simmer for 1½ hours, stirring once or twice.

Add the remaining 2 quarts cold water. Return to a boil over high heat. Reduce the heat to moderate and simmer 1½ to 2 hours, stirring occasionally. Remove from the heat and cool to room temperature. Skim the fat from the surface and discard, or save to use for cooking.

Strain the mixture through a colander set over a large pot or bowl. Separate the meat from the bones, taking care to discard any bits of cartilage, skin, or small bones from the meat. Save the meat for soup and discard the bones and vegetables. Transfer the strained stock to a nonreactive container with a tight-fitting lid. Store in the refrigerator for up to 5 days, or in the freezer for up to 4 months.

Carrots

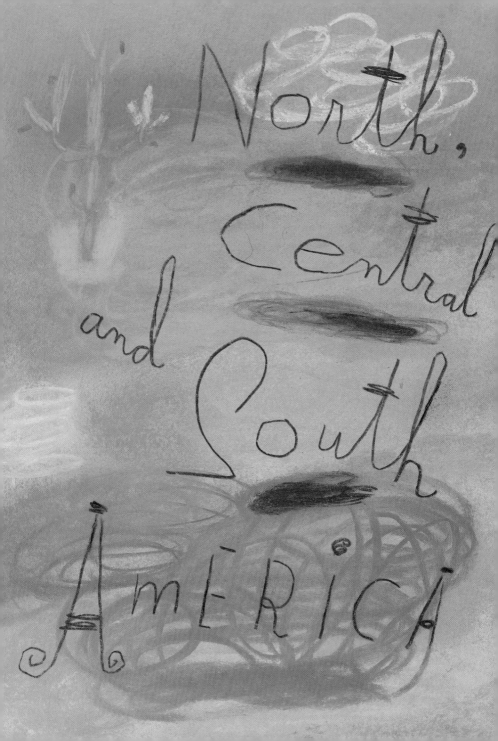

North, Central and South AMERICA

North, Central, and South America

From the hot, sultry regions of South and Central America and Mexico, to the cold New England states of North America, this chapter includes recipes both exotic and familiar; delicate and hearty; tropical in flavor and classically American in essence. This assortment is sure to please any palate.

The varied culinary styles of African- and European-influenced South America are presented here with soups from Brazil, Chile, Columbia, and Venezuela. Ingredients such as beef, fresh clams, hearts of palm, fresh fennel, capers, parsley, butter (rather than lard), olive oil, and of course, potatoes frequently appear in these dishes. Central American cuisine, closer in style to that of Mexico, is represented by Nicaraguan and Salvadorean soups that feature typical ingredients like sweet potatoes, corn, chili peppers, tomatoes, cilantro, and *masa harina*. Two Mexican recipes showcase such favored ingredients as fresh limes, chili peppers, and corn tortillas.

From regional North American cuisines, diverse in their own right, are soups from the Deep South, the Southwest, and New England, along with a classic recipe for "Jewish Penicillin." Regardless of region, the North American soups are typified by their use of fresh vegetables and ingredients that reflect the cuisines of the different ethnic groups that settle in this large geographic area.

These soups tend to be hearty and filling, ideal for using as a main meal, especially when combined with a salad and appropriate bread. The tempting recipes in this chapter encompass the diverse flavors of the Americas, and the many incarnations of chicken soup.

Mexican Chicken and Lime Soup

This traditional Mexican soup often includes fried corn tortillas, but this version, thickened with a little *masa harina*, is easier to prepare and less caloric. Drizzle with *crema* or sour cream, or serve with a *salsa fresca* made with fresh, ripe tomatoes, finely chopped onions, jalapeño peppers, and fresh cilantro.

MAKES ABOUT 10 CUPS.

2 large onions, quartered and cut into $1/2$-inch-wide slices
5 cloves garlic, finely chopped
2 teaspoons each dried oregano and ground coriander
3 tablespoons chicken fat or olive oil
9 cups Strong Chicken Stock (see page 20)
3 tablespoons masa harina *(Mexican corn flour)*
1 lime, quartered
2 green California or poblano chili peppers, stemmed,
    seeded, and cut into $1/2$-inch-wide squares
Juice from 5 limes (about $2/3$ cup fresh lime juice)
2 cups coarsely chopped, cooked white chicken meat
    (see page 13)
Salt and pepper, to taste
$3/4$ cup coarsely chopped fresh cilantro, for garnish
1 cup Mexican crema *or sour cream, for garnish*

In a heavy-bottomed, 4-quart saucepan, cook the onion, garlic, oregano, and coriander in the chicken fat over high heat for 5 to 7 minutes, stirring constantly, until the onions are light golden brown. Add the chicken stock and *masa harina* and bring to a boil over high heat. Cook for 5 minutes, stirring frequently.

Add the quartered lime, chilies, and lime juice and return to the boil. Reduce the heat to mod-erate and cook for 15 minutes. Remove and discard the lime. Add the chicken and cook for 5 minutes, stirring occasionally. Season with salt and pepper. Just before serving, garnish each portion with cilantro and drizzle with *crema* or sour cream.

Mexican Chicken Chili Pepper-Tortilla Soup

This rustic Mexican soup is good served with a swirl of sour cream or Mexican *crema*, or a tablespoon of crumbled fresh Mexican cheese. If you have leftover turkey, you can substitute it for the chicken in this recipe.

MAKES ABOUT 10 CUPS.

1 large onion, cut into medium dice
3 tablespoons olive or vegetable oil
8 cups Strong Chicken Stock (see page 20)
4 roasted Anaheim or California green chili peppers,
*   peeled, stemmed, seeded, and diced (see page 141)*
2½ cups finely chopped dark chicken meat
2 teaspoons dried oregano
6 corn tortillas, halved and cut into ¼-inch-wide strips
Salt and pepper, to taste
1 large tomato, cored and finely diced, for garnish
¾ cup chopped fresh cilantro, for garnish

In a heavy-bottomed, 4-quart saucepan, cook the onion in the olive oil over moderate heat for 10 minutes, stirring frequently. Add the stock, chilies, chicken, and oregano and bring to a boil over high heat. Reduce the heat to moderate and simmer for 15 minutes, or until the chicken is cooked through. Add the tortillas and cook 5 minutes. Season with salt and pepper. Garnish each portion with tomato and cilantro just before serving.

Salvadorean Chicken and Vegetable Soup

The natural goodness of this colorful soup is enhanced by a sprinkling of red onion and a squeeze of fresh lime juice. Pair with hot dinner rolls or warm tortillas and imported beer.

MAKES ABOUT 12 CUPS.

1 large onion, cut into medium dice
2 cloves garlic, minced
2 tablespoons chicken fat or vegetable oil
12 cups Strong Chicken Stock (see page 20)
2 teaspoons dried oregano
2 large sweet potatoes, peeled and cut into 1-inch cubes
3 cups shredded, cooked dark chicken meat (see page 13)
2 medium tomatoes, cored and coarsely chopped
2 small ears corn, shaved (about 1½ cups corn kernels)
Salt and pepper, to taste
1 cup chopped fresh cilantro, for garnish

In a heavy-bottomed, 6-quart saucepan, cook the onion and garlic in the chicken fat over moderate heat for 10 minutes, stirring frequently. Add the chicken stock and oregano and bring to a boil over high heat. Add the potatoes and reduce the heat to moderate. Cook for 15 minutes or until the potatoes are almost tender. Add the chicken, tomatoes, and corn and cook for 5 minutes. Season with salt and pepper. Garnish each portion with cilantro just before serving.

Chilean Chicken Soup with Fennel

This soup is traditionally made with yucca, but this version is made with fresh fennel and potatoes.

MAKES ABOUT, 10 CUPS.

*2 bulbs fennel, tough outer leaves discarded, cored,
   and cut into small dice*
2 medium new potatoes, cut into small dice
3 cloves garlic, minced
4 jalapeño chili peppers, stemmed, seeded, and minced
2 teaspoons fennel seeds, ground
3 tablespoons olive oil
½ cup dry sherry
8 cups Light Chicken Stock (see page 22)
3 cups finely chopped white chicken meat (see page 13)
4 medium tomatoes, cored and cut into small dice
Salt and pepper, to taste
⅓ cup minced fresh parsley, for garnish

In a heavy-bottomed, 4-quart saucepan, cook the fennel, potatoes, garlic, jalapeño peppers, and fennel seeds in the olive oil over high heat for 5 minutes, stirring constantly. Add the sherry and cook for 3 minutes or until it evaporates.

Add the stock and bring to a boil. Reduce the heat to moderately low and cook for 20 minutes or until the potatoes are tender. Add the chicken and tomatoes and cook for 5 minutes. Season with salt and pepper. Garnish each portion with parsley just before serving.

Brazilian
Chicken and Rice
SOUP.

hearts
of
palm

cilantro

Rogers

Brazilian Chicken and Rice Soup
with Hearts of Palm

Hot chili peppers and cayenne pepper contrast nicely with the mildly sweet flavors of fresh corn and coconut milk in this distinctive soup.

Hearts of palm can be found in the canned vegetable section of many upscale grocery stores or specialty food shops, but if you can't find this exotic vegetable, substitute whole bamboo shoots.

MAKES ABOUT 12 CUPS.

1 large onion, cut into small dice

2 cloves garlic, finely chopped

4 serrano or jalapeño chili peppers, stemmed and finely chopped

1 teaspoon ground allspice

½ teaspoon cayenne pepper

2 tablespoons unsalted butter

2 tablespoons olive oil

½ cup long-grain white rice

10 cups Light Chicken Stock (see page 22)

1 13½-ounce can unsweetened coconut milk

2 small ears corn, shaved (about 1½ cups corn kernels)

1 10-ounce can hearts of palm, drained and sliced into
½-inch pieces (about 1½ cups)

1½ cups coarsely chopped white chicken meat

Salt and pepper, to taste

½ cup coarsely chopped fresh cilantro, for garnish

In a heavy-bottomed, 4-quart saucepan, cook the onion, garlic, chili peppers, and spices in the butter and olive oil over moderate heat for 10 minutes, stirring frequently. Add the rice, chicken stock, and coconut milk and bring to a boil over high heat. Reduce the heat to moderate and cook 20 to 25 minutes, or until the rice is tender.

Add the corn, hearts of palm, and chicken and cook 10 minutes, stirring occasionally. Season with salt and pepper. Garnish each portion with cilantro just before serving.

Colombian Chicken and Potato Soup with Corn and Capers

Choose the larger Greek or Spanish capers for this unusual, rich and piquant South American soup. Served chilled, this dish would be wonderful paired with warm bread and perhaps a mixed green salad for a late-night summer dinner.

MAKES ABOUT 8 CUPS.

1 large onion, cut into small dice
3 tablespoons olive oil
2 teaspoons each dried oregano and sage
2 large boiling potatoes (about 1 pound), cut into small dice
6 cups Strong Chicken Stock (see page 20)
1 cup heavy cream
2 large ears corn, shaved (about 2 cups corn kernels)
2 cups finely chopped, cooked dark chicken meat (see page 13)
¼ cup capers
Salt and pepper, to taste

In a heavy-bottomed, 4-quart saucepan, cook the onion in the olive oil over moderately high heat for 5 minutes, stirring occasionally. Add the herbs, potatoes, chicken stock, and cream. Bring to a boil over high heat and cook for 5 minutes, stirring constantly to prevent the mixture from boiling over. Add the corn, chicken, and capers. Reduce the heat to moderate and cook for 5 minutes, stirring occasionally. Season with salt and pepper. Serve hot or chilled.

Nicaraguan Chicken Soup with Masa Harina Patties

This recipe is an adaptation of the classic Nicaraguan *Sopa de Rosquillas*, a soup traditionally served for the seven Fridays prior to Easter Sunday. In this version, the *masa harina* dough is formed into small patties rather than rings.

Masa harina, a Latin American corn flour, can be purchased in Latin food stores, many natural food shops, and most upscale grocery stores.

MAKES ABOUT 12 CUPS.

MASA HARINA PATTIES:
> 2 *cups* masa harina *(yellow corn flour)*
> *4 ounces sharp Cheddar cheese, finely grated*
> *2 tablespoons unsalted butter, room temperature*
> *1½ teaspoons kosher or sea salt*
> *½ to ⅔ cup cold water*
> *4 tablespoons light olive oil*

> *1 medium onion, cut into small dice*
> *3 cloves garlic, finely chopped*
> *4 jalapeño chili peppers, stemmed and coarsely chopped*
> *1 red bell pepper, stemmed, seeded, and cut into small dice*
> *3 tablespoons olive oil or chicken fat*
> *8 cups Strong Chicken Stock (see page 20)*
> *2½ cups finely shredded cooked dark chicken meat (see page 13)*
> *Salt and pepper, to taste*
> *½ cup coarsely chopped fresh cilantro, for garnish*

To make the *masa harina* patties: In a medium bowl, combine the *masa harina*, cheese, butter, and salt using your hands. Add enough of the water to hold the dough together. Form dough into a disc, cover with plastic wrap, and let stand at room temperature for 30 minutes. Divide the ball into 4 equal balls and roll each into a long cylinder approximately 1 inch thick. Cut each cylinder into 6 equal pieces and shape each into a small patty approximately ¼ inch thick.

In a large, nonstick saute pan, heat 2 tablespoons of the olive oil over moderate heat. When the oil is warm, add half of the patties. Cook about 1 minute on each side, or until both sides are light golden brown. Remove from the pan and place on a large plate. In the same manner, cook the rest of the patties in the remaining olive oil. Set aside.

In a heavy-bottomed, 6-quart saucepan, cook the onion, garlic, and jalapeño and bell peppers in the olive oil over moderate heat for 10 minutes, stirring frequently. Add the chicken stock and bring to a boil over high heat. Add the chicken and *masa* patties and reduce the heat to moderate. Simmer 5 to 7 minutes, or until the patties and chicken are warmed through. Season with salt and pepper. Garnish each portion with cilantro just before serving.

Venezuelan Chicken and Clam Soup

This particular South American dish, with its inclusion of seafood and beef, extends the traditional concept of chicken soup. The variety of protein-rich ingredients in this dish makes it not only delicious but nutritious as well. Although the clams add a unique flavor, the soup is still tasty without them.

MAKES ABOUT IO CUPS.

1 beef oxtail
3 chicken thighs
2 large carrots, cut into 1-inch chunks
2 stalks celery, cut into 1-inch chunks
1 large onion, coarsely chopped
2 teaspoons each dried oregano and ground cumin
5 quarts cold water
3 medium boiling potatoes (about 1 pound),
   cut into medium dice
2 cups finely shredded white cabbage
1 large ear corn, shaved (about 1 cup corn kernels)
24 small clams (about 2 pounds), cleaned and shells brushed
Salt and pepper, to taste
1 cup coarsely chopped fresh cilantro, for garnish

Place the beef, chicken, carrots, celery, onion, oregano, and cumin in an 8-quart saucepan. Add 3 quarts of the water and bring to a boil over high heat. Reduce the heat to moderate and cook for 1 hour, stirring from time to time. Add the remaining water and again bring to a boil. Reduce the heat to moderate and cook for 1 to 1½ hours, or until the beef is very tender and the chicken is thoroughly cooked.

Strain the mixture in a large colander set inside a large pot. Remove the chicken and beef; set aside. Using the back of a spoon, press the vegetables against the side of the colander to extract their juices into the liquid.

Remove the chicken from the bones; discard the bones and add the chicken to the liquid. Remove the bones and fat from the beef and discard. Add the beef to the liquid.

Add the potatoes to the chicken-beef mixture and cook over moderately high heat for 20 minutes or until they are tender. Add the cabbage, corn, and clams and cook for 2 to 3 minutes or until the clam shells have opened. Remove and discard any clams with closed shells. Mix the soup well, and season with salt and pepper. Garnish each portion with cilantro just before serving.

Manischewitz

ⓤ MATZO
MEAL
Net wt. 16 oz.

Chicken
SOUP
with
matzo
balls

Chicken Soup with Matzo Balls

In a class by itself, the recipe for matzo balls given here needs only a pot of rich, flavorful chicken broth to transform it into the queen of chicken soups.

If you cannot eat the soup right away, carefully remove the cooked matzo balls from the broth using a slotted spoon and place on a flat surface. Cool to room temperature. Wrap in plastic or foil and refrigerate for up to 2 days until ready to eat. To reheat matzo balls, bring the chicken stock to a boil over high heat. Add the cooked matzo balls, reduce the heat to moderately low and heat through, about 3 minutes. Serve immediately.

MAKES ABOUT 12 CUPS SOUP (16 MATZO BALLS).

MATZO BALLS:
>   3 large eggs, well beaten
>   ½ cup seltzer water
>   6 tablespoons chicken fat, melted and cooled
>   3 tablespoons finely minced onion
>   2½ teaspoons kosher salt
>   ½ teaspoon each white pepper and ground nutmeg
>   1¼ cups matzo meal
>
>   10 cups Strong Chicken Stock (see page 20)
>   ½ cup finely chopped fresh parsley, for garnish

To make the matzo ball batter: In a large bowl, combine the eggs, seltzer water, chicken fat, salt, pepper, and nutmeg; mix thoroughly.

Gradually stir in the matzo meal, gently mixing until all ingredients are just combined (do not overmix). The batter will be wet and loose at this point. Cover tightly and refrigerate for at least 3 hours or up to 8 hours.

In a 5-quart pot, bring the chicken stock to a boil over high heat. Reduce to moderate and cook 20 to 25 minutes while you form the matzo balls.

To form the batter into balls: Using about 2 tablespoons for each ball, form the dough into balls using moistened palms. When all the batter has been used, gently drop the matzo balls, three or four at a time, into the chicken stock. Cook 10 to 12 minutes, or until the matzo balls are cooked through. Season the soup with salt and pepper. Serve immediately garnished with the parsley.

Tex-Mex Smoked Chicken and Chili Pepper Soup

Dried chili peppers, smoked chicken, pinto beans, and spices and herbs indigenous to the southwestern United States make this sensational soup a terrific cold-weather dish for hearty appetites. Serve with warm corn tortillas, pan-fried flour tortillas, or cornbread.

Smoked chicken is preferable in this recipe, but a high-quality commercial barbecued chicken, purchased whole from your local barbecue joint, would also be fine. If these birds aren't available, a regular oven-roasted chicken can be used. Although I prefer using home-cooked dried beans, this soup has so many flavorful ingredients, canned pinto beans can be substituted if you are pressed for time. Add along with the chicken stock.

All of the ingredients for this recipe can be found in Latin markets, gourmet grocery stores, specialty food shops, and many natural food stores. Chipotle chili peppers are fresh jalapeño chili peppers that have been smoked and dried. Whether purchased dry in bulk form, pickled in jars, or combined with adobo sauce and packed in cans, chipotle chili peppers are undeniably one of the hottest, most flavorful chilies available.

MAKES ABOUT 11 CUPS.

½ cup dried pinto beans, washed and sorted
(about 1⅓ cups cooked pinto beans)
2 dried pasilla chili peppers
2 dried ancho chili peppers
1 or 2 dried chipotle chili peppers, to taste
10 cups Light Chicken Stock (see page 22)
1 large onion, cut into small dice
3 cloves garlic, finely chopped
3 tablespoons chicken fat or olive oil
2 teaspoons each dried sage, oregano, ground cumin,
and coriander
1 3- to 3½-pound smoked whole chicken, meat removed and
finely chopped (about 2 cups)
2 large green California or fresh poblano chili peppers,
stemmed, seeded, and cut into small dice
2 small chayote squash or green pattypan squash,
cut into medium dice
Salt and pepper, to taste
½ cup finely chopped fresh cilantro, for garnish

Soak the pinto beans in 4 cups of water overnight. Drain well and place in a medium saucepan with 6 cups fresh water. Bring to a boil over high heat. Reduce the heat to moderate and cook for 1½ hours, or until the beans are tender. Drain well and set aside.

Soak the dried chilies in cold water to cover for 1 to 2 hours or until soft and pliable. Remove the stems and seeds and discard. Place the dried chilies in a blender with 1 cup of the chicken stock. Puree until smooth. Set aside.

In a heavy-bottomed, 8-quart saucepan, cook the onion and garlic in the chicken fat over moderate heat for 10 minutes, stirring frequently. Add the herbs and spices, remaining chicken stock, reserved pureed chilies, and pinto beans; bring to a boil over high heat. Reduce the heat to moderate and cook for 30 minutes, stirring occasionally.

Add the chicken meat, fresh chili peppers, and squash (and canned pinto beans, if using) and cook for 12 to 15 minutes, or until the vegetables are tender but not mushy. Season with salt and pepper. Garnish each portion with cilantro just before serving.

New England Chicken and Bacon Soup

I adore the smokey flavors of bacon and sharp Cheddar cheese paired with chicken and creamy potatoes. This is an ideal soup to serve for a filling lunch on icy-cold days. For a rib-sticking dinner, serve with a spicy cabbage slaw and bread or crackers.

MAKES ABOUT 11 CUPS.

1 pound thick-sliced bacon, coarsely chopped

1 large onion, cut into medium dice

3 cloves garlic, finely chopped

1 cup light ale or beer

1½ teaspoons each paprika, celery seeds, and yellow
mustard seeds

3 rounded tablespoons all-purpose flour

9 cups Strong Chicken Stock (see page 20)

4 medium new potatoes (about 1⅓ pounds), halved lengthwise,
each piece halved and sliced into ¼-inch-thick pieces

1 cup heavy cream

⅔ pound sharp Cheddar cheese, grated

2½ cups coarsely chopped, cooked white chicken meat
(see page 13)

Salt and pepper, to taste

½ cup minced fresh parsley, for garnish

In a heavy-bottomed, 6-quart saucepan, cook the bacon over
moderate heat until crispy, removing with a slotted spoon when
done. Drain on paper towels. When cool, coarsely chop and set aside.

Remove all but ¼ cup of the bacon fat from the saucepan. (Discard
the remaining bacon fat or save to use in another recipe.) Cook the
onion and garlic in the bacon fat over moderately low heat for 10
minutes, stirring frequently. Add the beer and spices and cook for 5
to 7 minutes or until the liquid has evaporated. Add the flour and cook
for 3 to 5 minutes, stirring constantly. Add the chicken stock a little
at a time, whisking constantly with a wire whisk to form a smooth
mixture. When all the stock has been added, bring to a boil over high
heat, stirring constantly and scraping the bottom of the pan to remove
any bits of food. Boil for 10 minutes, stirring frequently.

Add the potatoes, cream, and reserved bacon. Reduce the heat to moderate and cook for 15 minutes, or until the potatoes are tender. Add the cheese and chicken and cook for 3 to 5 minutes, or until the chicken is heated through and all the cheese has melted. Season with salt and pepper. Garnish each portion with parsley just before serving.

Louisiana Chicken Gumbo

There are probably just as many versions of this dish in Louisiana as there are fine Louisiana cooks, but this rendition ranks as one of my all-time favorite soups. This potage, filled with a colorful variety of vegetables and meat, is best when prepared with fresh vegetables, but in the dead of winter, I find frozen okra, lima beans, and even corn acceptable.

Filé powder—young, dried and ground sassafras leaves—is used to flavor and thicken gumbos. It should be added just before serving, rather than during cooking, as it becomes stringy and gooey when heated for prolonged periods of time. For this reason, add it only to the amount of soup being served immediately, or omit it entirely. The amount given below is enough for the entire pot of soup.

MAKES ABOUT 11 CUPS.

1 large onion, cut into small dice

3 cloves garlic, finely chopped

2 jalapeño chili peppers, stemmed and finely chopped

2 tablespoons olive oil

3 tablespoons chicken fat or olive oil

4 tablespoons all-purpose flour

8 cups Strong Chicken Stock (see page 20)

1 tablespoon dried thyme

1 cup fresh cooked or frozen lima beans

½ pound okra, stemmed and sliced into ½-inch rounds
    (about 1 cup)

2 large ears corn, shaved (about 2 cups corn kernels)

1 green bell pepper, stemmed, seeded, and cut into small dice

4 medium ripe tomatoes, cored and cut into medium dice

½-pound slice smoked ham, cut into small dice (about 2 cups)

2 cups coarsely chopped white chicken meat

Salt and pepper, to taste

6 tablespoons filé powder (optional)

In a heavy-bottomed, 6-quart saucepan, cook the onion, garlic, and jalapeño peppers in the olive oil and chicken fat over moderate heat for 10 minutes, stirring frequently. Add the flour and cook for 5 minutes, stirring constantly. Add the chicken stock a little at a time, and whisk to make a smooth mixture. When all the stock has been added, add the thyme and bring to a boil over high heat, stirring constantly. Boil for 5 to 7 minutes, stirring frequently and scraping the bottom of the pan.

Add the lima beans, okra, corn, bell pepper, tomatoes, and ham. Reduce the heat to moderate and cook 25 to 30 minutes, stirring occasionally. Add the chicken and cook 5 minutes, or just until the chicken is cooked through. Season with salt and pepper. Add the filé powder, heat for 1 minute, and serve immediately.

Asia

and

the

South

PACIFIC

ASIA AND THE SOUTH PACIFIC

This chapter, centered around the soups of Asia, includes many popular, familiar recipes as well as a few lesser-known dishes that promise to intrigue and delight. Drawn from Thailand and Vietnam, the South Pacific island of Tahiti, the Philippines, Indonesia, Hawaii, and China, these recipes illustrate the wide variety of cooking styles and ingredients indigenous to this part of the world.

Lemongrass, shallots, fresh basil and mint, coconut milk, and fish sauce are just a few of the Southeast Asian ingredients used in these recipes. Rice, noodles, fresh vegetables, and in a few cases, barbecued pork and ham appear in the Chinese and Filipino dishes, and fresh papaya is called for in the Tahitian chicken soup. An abundance of spices and fresh herbs is evident throughout.

Asian grocery stores are the best source for Asian and South Pacific ingredients. However, many specialty, gourmet, ethnic, and natural food stores also carry basic Asian foodstuffs, as do some upscale and full-service grocery stores. Cross-cultural food items such as dried shrimp and mushrooms, fresh and dried chili peppers, fresh and canned tropical fruits and vegetables, and whole spices and fresh herbs are often available in Latin food markets.

These soups, which cover the range from light and refreshing to robust and filling, have bright flavors and stimulating textures. Don't be put off by the recipes with many ingredients. In many cases, these lists are comprised largely of spices and other flavoring ingredients that require no preparation—the process is simple and the results are sensational.

Vietnamese Creamed Corn and Chicken Soup

Although fresh corn is available in many parts of Vietnam, creamed corn—introduced by the French—is preferable in this rich dish.

MAKES ABOUT 11 CUPS.

2 stalks lemongrass, outer leaves removed
5 shallots, thinly sliced
4 cloves garlic, thinly sliced
2 serrano chili peppers, stemmed and thinly sliced
3 tablespoons peanut oil
6 cups Light Chicken Stock (see page 22)
2 16-ounce cans creamed corn
3 tablespoons fish sauce (nuoc cham)
2 cups shredded, cooked dark chicken meat (see page 13)
1 small bunch green onions, finely chopped
White pepper, to taste
½ cup chopped fresh cilantro

Using a sharp knife, cut across the lemongrass stalks approximately ½ inch from the root end. Cut off the green stalks leaving the hard pale portion. Slice into thin rounds.

In a heavy-bottomed, 4-quart saucepan, cook the lemongrass, shallots, garlic, and chilies in the peanut oil over high heat for 5 minutes, stirring constantly. Add the chicken stock, corn, and fish sauce and bring to a boil over high heat. Reduce the heat to moderately high and cook 10 minutes. Add the chicken and green onions and cook 3 to 5 minutes. Season with white pepper. Garnish each portion with cilantro just before serving.

Thai Coconut-Curry Chicken Soup

Like many Asian dishes, this soup has a rather long list of ingredients, but the preparation is actually simple and straightforward, and amply rewarding. If you can't find the small, round, cream-colored Thai eggplants, then use the slender Japanese, Chinese, or Italian varieties.

MAKES ABOUT 12 CUPS.

3 cloves garlic, thinly sliced

3 serrano chili peppers, stemmed and thinly sliced

2 teaspoons each ground coriander and turmeric

1 teaspoon each ground caraway seeds, anise, and white peppercorns

½ teaspoon ground cloves

2 tablespoons peanut oil

10 cups Light Chicken Stock (see page 20)

2 14-ounce cans unsweetened coconut milk

Grated zest from 2 limes

2 tablespoons fish sauce (nuoc cham)

1 pound Thai or Japanese eggplants, halved and cut into 1-inch chunks

3 cups coarsely chopped white chicken meat

1 tablespoon sugar

½ cup each coarsely chopped fresh cilantro and basil

In a heavy-bottomed, 6-quart saucepan, saute the garlic, chilies, and spices in the peanut oil over moderate heat for 10 minutes, stirring frequently. Add the chicken stock, coconut milk, lime zest, and fish sauce. Bring to a boil over high heat and cook for 10 minutes, stirring occasionally. Add the eggplant, chicken, and sugar, reduce the heat to moderately low, and simmer for 12 to 15 minutes or until the eggplant is very tender and the chicken is just cooked through. Garnish each portion with cilantro and basil just before serving.

Thai Spicy Lemongrass Chicken Soup

This Thai soup is light and refreshing, yet spicy and pungent. It is a fine soup to make during the summer months when tomatoes and zucchini are at their peak.

Lovers of incendiary foods may enjoy eating the small, dried chili peppers in this dish, but those with sensitive palates ought to avoid them. Either extract the dried chili peppers from the soup before serving, or allow your guests to remove, avoid, or consume them as they wish.

MAKES ABOUT II CUPS.

4 lemongrass stalks, outer leaves removed
5 shallots, thinly sliced
4 cloves garlic, thinly sliced
6-inch piece fresh ginger root, peeled and thinly sliced
4 serrano chili peppers, stemmed and thinly sliced
3 tablespoons peanut oil
12 cups Strong Chicken Stock (see page 20)
8 small dried red chili peppers
3 tablespoons fish sauce (nuoc cham)
1½ tablespoons sugar
Juice from 2 limes
4 small zucchini, halved and cut into ½-inch half-moons
2 medium tomatoes, cored and coarsely chopped
2½ cups coarsely chopped, cooked dark chicken meat
  (see page 13)
½ cup each coarsely chopped fresh basil and cilantro

Using a sharp knife, make a cut across the lemongrass stalk approximately ½ inch from the root end, and just above the hard, pale bottom portion. Discard the root. Thinly slice the 2-inch piece into thin rounds and save the long pieces for cooking in the soup.

In a heavy-bottomed, 6-quart saucepan, cook the sliced lemongrass, shallots, garlic, ginger, and chilies in the peanut oil over moderate heat for 5 minutes, stirring constantly. Add the chicken stock, dried chilies, fish sauce, sugar, and long pieces of lemongrass and bring to a boil over high heat. Add the lime juice, zucchini, tomatoes, and chicken. Reduce the heat to moderately low, and simmer for 5 to 7 minutes or until the vegetables are tender but not mushy. Remove the long pieces of lemongrass and discard. Garnish each portion with basil and cilantro just before serving.

Chinese Sizzling Rice Chicken Soup

Traditional sizzling rice soup also includes beef and prawns, but this simple version depends on a strong, homemade chicken stock, tender dark chicken meat, and green peas for its appealing flavor.

One of the secrets to making sizzling rice soup is the rice—it must be completely dry before deep-frying and adding to the stock. Most Chinese restaurants add the sizzling rice to the soup at the table. To make the same dramatic presentation, you must coordinate the last-minute cooking of the rice with the addition of the snow peas and cabbage to the broth—both the rice and the liquid must be very hot or the rice won't sizzle. Cook the rice for a couple of minutes in the hot vegetable oil before adding the snow peas and cabbage to the broth. Most likely the rice will be crispy and the vegetables *al dente* if you follow these step-by-step directions.

MAKES ABOUT 12 CUPS.

1 cup long-grain white rice
10 cups Strong Chicken Stock (see page 20)
3-inch piece ginger root, peeled and finely chopped
3 cloves garlic, finely chopped
2 tablespoons soy sauce
2 cups shredded, cooked dark chicken meat (see page 13)
Salt and ground Szechwan or black pepper, to taste
2 cups vegetable oil, for frying
¼ head Napa or savoy cabbage, finely shredded (about 3 cups)
1½ cups shelled fresh or frozen green peas

Preheat oven to 300°F.

Place 3 quarts of water in a 5-quart saucepan. Bring to a boil over high heat. Add the rice and mix well. Return to the boil and cook 7 to 10 minutes, stirring occasionally, until the rice is tender but not mushy. Drain thoroughly in a colander with small holes or a sieve. Arrange the rice in a single layer on a baking sheet and cool to room temperature. When the rice is cool and dry, bake in the oven for 20 to 30 minutes, or until each kernel is dry and crisp. Remove from the oven and cool to room temperature. Set aside.

Place the chicken stock, ginger, garlic, soy sauce, and chicken in a heavy-bottomed, 6-quart saucepan. Bring to a boil over high heat. Reduce the heat to moderate and cook 10 minutes, stirring occasionally. Season with salt and pepper.

Heat the vegetable oil in a heavy-bottomed, 2-quart saucepan over high heat. When the oil is hot but not smoking, add the reserved rice and cook 5 to 7 minutes, or until the rice is very crispy and barely golden brown.

While the rice cooks, add the cabbage and peas to the chicken stock and cook for 5 minutes. Remove the rice from the oil with a slotted spoon and place on a heated platter. Carefully lower the sizzling-hot rice into the hot soup. Serve immediately.

Chinese Chicken-Wonton Soup

Don't be daunted by the lengthy directions—once you make one or two wontons and get the hang of it, the rest will be effortless. Since it takes the same amount of time to prepare the filling, and just a few additional minutes to fold them, double the recipe for wontons when preparing this soup. Use half the wontons in the soup, and freeze the remaining half by first placing them in a single layer on a baking sheet and freezing until hard. Carefully place the frozen wontons in a double-thick, airtight plastic bag, seal tightly, and place inside another plastic bag. Label and date the package. Wontons will keep in the freezer for up to 6 months.

MAKES ABOUT 12 CUPS.

WONTONS:

1 whole chicken breast, skin, bones, and cartilage removed,
   coarsely chopped (about 1 cup)
¼ pound bacon, coarsely chopped
½ bunch green onions, coarsely chopped (about ¾ cup)
1 tablespoon soy sauce
1 tablespoon seasoned rice wine vinegar
½ teaspoon kosher salt
¼ teaspoon ground Szechwan or black pepper
¼ cup cornstarch
¼ cup cold water
½ 16-ounce package wonton skins (about 60 skins)

12 cups Strong Chicken Stock (see page 20)
1 small zucchini, julienned
Salt and pepper, to taste

To make the wontons: Place the chicken, bacon, green onions, soy sauce, vinegar, salt, and pepper in a food processor. Process until finely minced and all ingredients are thoroughly mixed. Transfer to a small, nonreactive bowl, cover, and refrigerate for at least 2 hours or up to 1 day.

Make a slurry by combining the cornstarch and the water in a small bowl; mix well.

To assemble the wontons: Arrange 12 wonton skins, each set on its point in the diamond position, on a flat surface. Using a pastry brush, lightly moisten each skin with the slurry, taking care to cover the entire surface. Place 1 rounded teaspoon of filling on the lower corner portion of each skin, leaving a ¼-inch border between the filling and the edges of the skins.

For each wonton, fold the top point of the skin over the bottom point, forming a triangle. Gently press the skins together, starting from the filling and going out toward the edges, squeezing the air out as you go. Moisten one of the side points with the slurry. Bring the two side points together, up over the filling, and seal tightly. Make the remaining wontons in this fashion, placing them spaced apart on a sheet pan. The wontons can be refrigerated for up to 30 minutes at this point, but if you can't use them before that time, or for those you plan to freeze for later use, it's best to place them directly in the freezer.

Place the chicken stock in a heavy-bottomed, 6-quart saucepan. Bring to a boil over high heat. Cook for 10 minutes, stirring occasionally. Add the zucchini and wontons. Reduce the heat to moderate and simmer gently for 3 minutes, or until the wontons are thoroughly cooked. Season with salt and pepper and serve immediately.

Filipino Chicken and Asparagus Soup with Ham

Unlike many other soups, this recipe does not require sautéing the ingredients before adding the stock. Simple yet rewarding, this easy-to-prepare dish is ideal for a light lunch. Fresh asparagus is terrific in this soup, but if you're making this recipe in the fall or winter, substitute fresh snow peas, which are usually available year-round. To prepare the snow peas, trim, remove the strings, and slice into ½-inch-wide pieces.

MAKES ABOUT 9 CUPS.

8 cups Strong Chicken Stock (see page 20)
3 tablespoons cornstarch
½ cup dry sherry
2 small bunches thin asparagus (about 1½ pounds), trimmed and cut on the diagonal into ½-inch-long pieces
½-pound slice of smoked ham, minced (about 2 cups)
2 cups slivered white chicken meat
Salt and white pepper, to taste

Place the stock in a heavy-bottomed, 4-quart saucepan. Bring to a boil over high heat. In a small bowl, mix the cornstarch with the sherry. Add to the stock and return to the boil. Cook for 5 to 7 minutes, stirring occasionally.

Add the asparagus, ham, and chicken and return to the boil. Cook for 3 to 5 minutes, or until the chicken is just cooked through and the asparagus is bright green. Season with salt and pepper and serve immediately.

poppy seeds

anchoviES

peAnuts

cilantro

ginger root

Indonesian Yellow Curry Chicken Soup

A complex mixture of spices combined with fresh ginger, hot chilies, garlic, onion, and peanuts makes this one of the more unique, spicy, and fiery selections in this book.

MAKES ABOUT 11 CUPS.

CURRY PASTE:

> 1 small onion, cut into small dice
> 5 cloves garlic, coarsely chopped
> 3 to 4 jalapeño chili peppers, stemmed and coarsely chopped
> 4 to 5 small dried red chili peppers, stemmed and coarsely chopped
> 4-inch piece fresh ginger root, peeled and thinly sliced
> 3 tablespoons unsweetened shredded coconut
> 3 tablespoons poppy seeds
> 2 teaspoons each turmeric and ground caraway seeds
> 1 teaspoon each ground cloves and mace
> 3 tablespoons plus 1/2 cup peanut oil
> 1 2-ounce tin anchovies, drained
> 1/2 cup roasted peanuts, coarsely chopped
> 1/2 cup water

> 10 cups Light Chicken Stock (see page 22)
> 3 medium boiling potatoes (about 1 lb.), cut into medium dice
> 2 small zucchini, halved and cut into 1/2-inch-wide half-moons
> 2 cups chopped, cooked white chicken meat (see page 13)
> Salt and pepper, to taste
> 1/2 cup coarsely chopped fresh cilantro, for garnish
> 1/2 cup coarsely chopped roasted peanuts, for garnish
> 2 hard-cooked eggs, coarsely chopped, for garnish

To make the curry paste: In a medium saute pan, cook the onion, galic, chili peppers, ginger, coconut, poppy seeds, and spices in 3 tablespoons of the peanut oil over high heat for 3 minutes, stirring constantly. Remove from the heat and cool slightly. Place the mixture in a blender along with the anchovies, peanuts, remaining ½ cup peanut oil, and the water. Grind until the mixture is smooth.

Transfer the curry paste to a heavy-bottomed, 4-quart saucepan. Add the chicken stock and bring to a boil over high heat, stirring frequently. Reduce the heat to moderate and cook for 15 minutes, stirring occasionally. Add the potatoes and cook for 10 minutes, or until tender. Add the zucchini and chicken and cook for 2 minutes, or until the zucchini is just tender. Season with salt and pepper. Just before serving, garnish each portion with cilantro, peanuts, and eggs.

Make me a cup of soup, please, Mommy

Hawaiian Chicken and Barbecued Pork Soup

A symphony of compatible sweet and savory ingredients comes together in this interesting soup, resulting in a medley of flavors and contrasting textures. Chinese-style barbecued pork, available in most Chinese take-out stores and restaurants, is best for this South Pacific dish, but if you can't find this variety, use the deboned meat from American-style barbecued pork ribs.

MAKES ABOUT 10 CUPS.

8 cups Strong Chicken Stock (see page 20)
2 tablespoons soy sauce
1 cup thinly sliced water chestnuts
¾ pound barbecued boneless Chinese-style pork shoulder,
   trimmed of excess fat and minced (about 2 cups)
2 cups diced, cooked dark chicken meat (see page 13)
1 large bunch green onions, finely chopped
Salt and pepper, to taste
1 small head Napa or savoy cabbage, trimmed, halved, and cut
   into ¼-inch-wide strips (about 2½ cups)

Place the chicken stock and soy sauce in a heavy-bottomed, 4-quart saucepan. Bring to a boil over high heat and cook for 3 to 5 minutes. Add the water chestnuts, pork, chicken, and green onions. Reduce the heat and cook for 5 minutes. Season with salt and pepper. Stir in the cabbage just before serving.

Tahitian Chicken-Papaya Soup

Three to four times larger than the familiar sweet, soft, orange-fleshed variety, green papayas have firm, crisp, pale yellow flesh with a mild, almost tart flavor. Favored in Southeast Asian, South American, and Caribbean cooking, uncooked green papayas are frequently used in salads and condiments; cooked, they appear in soups, stews, and stir-fried dishes. Both the green and orange-fleshed papaya grow in hot, tropical countries.

If you can't find a green cooking papaya, use an unripe, green-skinned eating papaya or a half-and-half mixture of grated carrot and peeled green apple.

MAKES 12 CUPS.

1 large onion, cut into small dice
4 serrano or jalapeño chili peppers, stemmed and finely chopped
3 tablespoons peanut oil
12 cups Light Chicken Stock (see page 22)
½ cup shredded unsweetened coconut
1 large green papaya, peeled, seeded, quartered, and thinly sliced (about 3 cups)
2½ cups coarsely chopped white chicken meat
Salt and pepper, to taste
1 large bunch watercress, stemmed and coarsely chopped

In a heavy-bottomed, 3-quart saucepan, cook the onion and chili peppers in the peanut oil over moderate heat for 10 minutes, stirring frequently. Add the chicken stock and coconut and bring to a boil over high heat. Cook 5 minutes, stirring occasionally. Add the papaya, reduce the heat to moderate, and cook 10 minutes, or until the papaya is tender. Add the chicken and cook 2 minutes, or until the chicken is just cooked through. Season with salt and pepper. Stir in the watercress just before serving.

free-range chicken

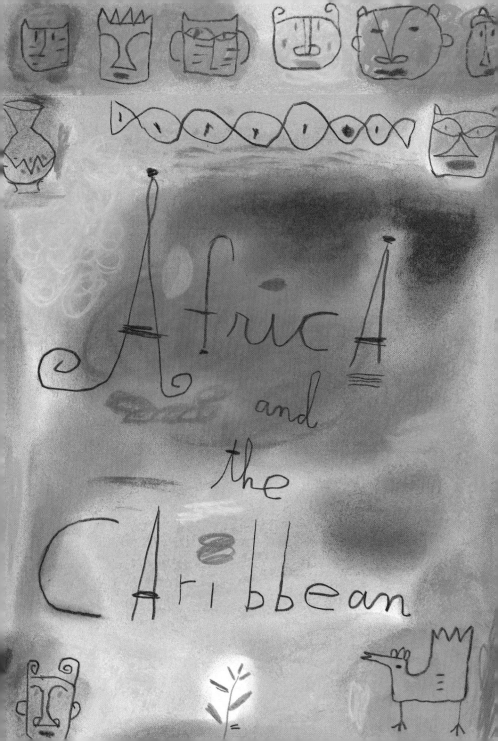

Africa and the Caribbean

Africa and the Caribbean

Although the African diet has changed over the centuries, certain mainstays prevail. Legumes and grains play a large role in African cooking, as do fresh vegetables such as corn, tomatoes, hot and mild peppers, onions, garlic, and, in certain areas, starchy root vegetables. Watermelon, plums, figs, and dates are also abundant. Small amounts of fresh meats, poultry, fish, and seafood are used in combination with fresh vegetables, grains, and starches to form complete, well-rounded meals. Spices and herbs are integral to this cuisine, lending both familiar and exotic tones to a myriad of African dishes.

Similarities between the culinary practices of Africa and the Caribbean can be attributed, in part, to slave trade between the two areas. The link between them, supported by the application of similar foodstuffs and cooking styles, further connects African cookery with that of the Caribbean.

The Caribbean, with its multiethnic background, is a true study in gustatory diversity. In addition to its African roots, we see French, Italian, Dutch, British, Indian, Chinese, and Spanish influences. Ingredients, cooking styles, and traditional foods have combined to form a wild patchwork of wonderful and delicious dishes. Winter squash, plantains, tomatoes, ginger, onions, garlic, and lots of hot chilies appear in many of these recipes, both Caribbean and African, as do various nuts, dried beans, cheeses, and a wondrous number of spices and herbs. The following recipes are some of the more exotic and compelling of this collection.

African Groundnut and Chicken Soup

Peanuts, often referred to as "groundnuts" in African cuisine, are a common ingredient in many soups and stews. In this hearty recipe, they lend richness, flavor, and protein, as well as a luscious texture. Make this robust soup in cold weather for a large group of adventurous friends.

MAKES ABOUT 11 CUPS.

4 chicken thighs
4 chicken legs
6-inch piece fresh ginger root, peeled and thinly sliced
8 cups Light Chicken Stock (see page 22)
8 cups water
3 tablespoons tomato paste
1 large onion, cut into small dice
3 jalapeño chili peppers, stemmed and minced
1 tablespoon ground coriander
1½ teaspoons ground mace
3 tablespoons peanut oil
2 medium tomatoes, cored and coarsely chopped
1 small eggplant, cut into small dice
½ pound fresh okra, stemmed and sliced into ½-inch rounds
    (about 1 cup)
⅔ cup chunky natural peanut butter
Salt and pepper, to taste

Place the chicken thighs, legs, ginger, stock, and water in a heavy-bottomed, 6-quart saucepan. Bring to a boil over high heat. Reduce the heat to moderate and cook for 1 hour. Remove the chicken with a slotted spoon and place in a colander. Cool to room temperature. When cool enough to handle, remove the meat from the bones, discard the bones, cartilage, and skin (or save for stock) and set the meat aside. Strain the stock in a colander or sieve and set aside.

In the same saucepan, cook the tomato paste, onion, jalapeños, and spices in the peanut oil over moderate heat for 7 minutes, stirring constantly. Add the tomatoes, eggplant, and okra and cook for 7 minutes, stirring frequently. Add the reserved stock and chicken and the peanut butter and bring to a boil over high heat. Reduce the heat to moderate and cook for 7 to 10 minutes or until the eggplant is tender and the liquid is smooth. Season with salt and pepper.

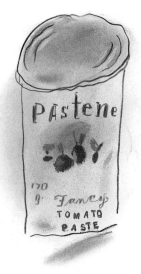

African Spicy chicken Soup with Plantains

ground
Coriander
cumin
cAyenne
tumeric

two
Jalepeno
chili peppers
four
Serrano
chili peppers

Anise
pimpinella
anisum

African Spicy Chicken Soup with Plantains

An intricate spice blend paired with plantains, hot chili peppers, and tender chunks of chicken results in a bold-tasting and satisfying soup.

Plantains are sold in ethnic markets that carry Latin, Caribbean, African, and in some instances, Asian produce. If you can't find plantains, use under-ripe bananas instead.

MAKES ABOUT 10 CUPS.

2 chicken thighs
2 chicken legs
2 chicken wings
5 quarts Light Chicken Stock (see page 22)
1 large onion, cut into medium dice
2 cloves garlic, finely chopped
4 serrano chili peppers, stemmed and coarsely chopped
2 jalapeño chili peppers, stemmed and coarsely chopped
1 tablespoon each ground coriander, cumin, and cayenne pepper
2 teaspoons each ground fenugreek, anise, and turmeric
6 tablespoons unsalted butter
2 plantains or green bananas, peeled, and coarsely chopped
2 stalks celery, trimmed and sliced on the diagonal
    into ½-inch pieces
1 cup unsweetened shredded coconut
Salt and pepper, to taste

Place the chicken thighs, legs, and wings in a heavy-bottomed, 6-quart saucepan. Add the chicken stock and bring to a boil over high heat. Reduce the heat to moderate and cook for 1 hour or until the chicken is tender. Remove chicken with a slotted spoon and place in a colander. Make sure no chicken bones remain in the liquid. When cool enough to handle, remove the meat from the bones, leaving it in large pieces, and set aside. Discard the bones, cartilage, and skin, or save for making stock.

In a large saute pan, cook the onion, garlic, chili peppers, and spices in the butter over moderately high heat for 5 to 7 minutes, stirring constantly. Add to the chicken stock, along with the plantains, celery, coconut, and reserved chicken. Bring to a boil over high heat. Reduce the heat to moderate and cook for 20 minutes, or until the plantains and celery are tender. Season with salt and pepper.

cup
of
Spicy
Soup.

East African Chicken Soup with Collard Greens

When combined with sweet-savory spices and the rich flavor of butter, common carrots and collard greens are transformed into something unforgettable. This soup takes less than 45 minutes to prepare, and is delicious when spiked with hot chili sauce and served with warm bread.

MAKES ABOUT 8 CUPS.

2 medium onions, cut into medium dice
5 cloves garlic, finely chopped
1 tablespoon ground coriander
2 teaspoons cayenne pepper
1½ teaspoons each ground cloves, allspice, and mace
4 tablespoons unsalted butter
6 cups Strong Chicken Stock (see page 20)
2 medium carrots, cut into ½-inch rounds
3 cups coarsely chopped, cooked dark chicken meat (see page 13)
1 bunch collard greens, stemmed, leaves halved and cut into
  ½-inch-wide ribbons (about 4 cups shredded greens)
Salt and pepper, to taste

In a heavy-bottomed, 4-quart saucepan, cook the onions, garlic, and spices in the butter over moderate heat for 5 to 7 minutes, stirring frequently. Add the stock and bring to a boil over high heat. Reduce the heat to moderate and cook for 30 minutes, stirring occasionally. Add the carrots and cook 7 to 10 minutes or until they are almost tender. Add the chicken and collard greens and cook 3 to 5 minutes or until the greens have just wilted. Season with salt and pepper.

Cuban Chicken and Black Bean Soup

Black beans, a classic Cuban ingredient, are often included in soups and stews or simply combined with onions and peppers and served over rice. The following recipe, which includes chicken meat, is a soup version of one of my favorite Caribbean black bean dishes. I like to spike the finished product with bottled hot sauce at the table.

MAKES ABOUT 6 CUPS.

1 cup dried black beans, sorted and washed
1 large smoked ham hock, cut into quarters
2 bay leaves
1 large onion, cut into small dice
3 cloves garlic, minced
3 jalapeño chili peppers, stemmed and minced
3 tablespoons olive oil
⅓ cup dark rum
2 cups diced white chicken meat
1 large bunch green onions, minced
Salt and pepper, to taste
½ cup chopped fresh cilantro, for garnish

Soak the beans overnight in 6 cups cold water. Drain well and set aside until needed. Place 5 quarts of water, the ham hock, and bay leaves in a heavy-bottomed, 8-quart saucepan. Bring to a boil over high heat. Reduce the heat to moderate and cook, stirring occasionally, for 1½ hours, or until the ham hock meat is very tender and falling from the bone. Add the soaked beans and bring to a boil over high heat. Reduce the heat to moderate and cook for 45 minutes, or until the beans are very tender.

In a saute pan, cook the onions, garlic, and chili peppers in the olive oil over moderate heat for 10 minutes, stirring frequently. Add to the cooked beans, along with the rum. Cook for 10 minutes longer. Add the chicken and green onions and cook for 5 to 7 minutes or until the chicken is just cooked through. Season with salt and pepper. Garnish each portion with cilantro just before serving.

Bantam Chicken

Cuban Sweet and Spicy Chicken and Squash Soup

The intriguing combination of plantains, squash, and apple juice makes this creamy-spicy soup a prizewinner.

MAKES ABOUT 11 CUPS.

1 large onion, coarsely chopped
4 red jalapeño chili peppers, stemmed and coarsely chopped
1 tablespoon ground coriander
2 teaspoons each ground cumin and mace
3 tablespoons olive oil
7 ½ cups Light Chicken Stock (see page 22)
1 ½ cups apple juice
1 large plantain or green banana, peeled and coarsely chopped
½ small winter squash, peeled, seeded, and coarsely chopped
    (about 2 cups chopped squash)
2 cups diced, cooked white chicken meat (see page 13)
Salt and pepper, to taste
½ cup minced fresh parsley, for garnish

In a heavy-bottomed, 4-quart saucepan, cook the onion, chilies, and spices in the olive oil over high heat for 5 minutes, stirring constantly. Add the stock, apple juice, plantain, and squash; bring to a boil. Reduce the heat to moderate and cook for 20 minutes, or until the vegetables are tender. Cool slightly.

In a blender, puree the mixture until smooth. Return to the saucepan and bring to a boil, stirring frequently. Add chicken and cook 3 minutes. Season with salt and pepper. Garnish with parsley just before serving.

Chicken-Vegetable Soup from Aruba

This outstanding recipe may have an intimidating list of ingredients, but there are only three steps necessary to create this nutritious and colorful recipe. Inspired by my travels to the Dutch West Indies, this soup is as visually appealing as it is good to eat.

MAKES ABOUT 16 CUPS.

4 chicken thighs
4 chicken legs
1 tablespoon dried thyme
12 cups Light Chicken Stock (see page 22)
4 cups water
2 medium red boiling potatoes (about ⅔ pound), cut into
    medium dice
2 small yams, peeled and cut into medium dice
½ small pumpkin, peeled, seeded, and cut into medium dice
    (about 4 cups diced pumpkin)
4 serrano chili peppers, stemmed and thinly sliced
4 roasted jalapeño chili peppers, stemmed, seeded, and
    coarsely chopped (see page 141)
1 cup fresh or frozen green peas
2 large ears corn, shaved (about 2 cups corn kernels)
4 medium tomatoes, cored and cut into large dice
Salt and pepper, to taste
Chopped olives and capers, for garnish (optional)

Place the chicken thighs, legs, thyme, 8 cups of the chicken stock, and 4 cups water in a heavy-bottomed, 6-quart saucepan. Bring to a boil over high heat. Reduce the heat to moderate and cook for 1 hour or until the chicken is tender. Skim the surface with a large spoon to remove the frothy foam, if necessary. Remove the chicken with a slotted spoon and place in a colander. Cool to room temperature. When cool, remove the meat from the bones and set aside. Save the bones, cartilage, and skin for stock or discard.

Add the remaining chicken stock to the chicken cooking liquid, along with the potatoes, yams, pumpkin, and chilies. Bring to a boil over high heat. Reduce the heat to moderate and cook for 10 minutes, stirring occasionally. Add the peas, corn, tomatoes, and reserved chicken and cook for 10 minutes. Season with salt and pepper. Garnish each portion with olives and capers just before serving, if desired.

Puerto Rican Chicken-Rice Soup with Peppers

This basic chicken soup, with its obvious Spanish overtones, is a restorative mélange that is sure to gratify.

MAKES ABOUT 10 CUPS.

1 large onion, cut into small dice
3 cloves garlic, minced
2 habanero chili peppers, stemmed and minced
2 jalapeño chili peppers, stemmed and minced
2 teaspoons each dried thyme and oregano
3 tablespoons olive oil
½ cup long-grain white rice
12 cups Strong Chicken Stock (see page 20)
4 tomatoes, cored and coarsely chopped
1 green bell pepper, stemmed, seeded, and cut into small dice
1 red bell pepper, stemmed, seeded, and cut into small dice
2 cups diced, cooked dark chicken meat (see page 13)
Salt and pepper, to taste
1 small bunch green onions, minced, for garnish

In a heavy-bottomed, 6-quart saucepan, cook the onion, garlic, chilies, and herbs in the olive oil over moderate heat for 5 minutes, stirring constantly. Add the rice and cook for 2 minutes, stirring constantly. Add the stock and bring to a boil over high heat. Reduce heat to moderate. Cook for 10 to 15 minutes or until rice is tender. Add tomatoes, peppers, and chicken. Cook for 7 to 10 minutes or until peppers are tender. Season with salt and pepper. Garnish each portion with green onions just before serving.

hibiscus

Jamaican
RED bean
chili-Pepper
chicken soup

red
beans

pink
BEANS

Jamaican Red Bean and Chili Pepper Chicken Soup

Hearty and spicy, this recipe is particularly good when prepared with smoked chicken or turkey. To extend this soup, spoon it over cooked rice or steamed new potatoes.

MAKES ABOUT 8 CUPS.

1 cup small dried red or pink beans, sorted and washed
10 cups Light Chicken Stock (see page 22)
1½ teaspoons each ground allspice and dried thyme
1 large onion, cut into small dice
3 cloves garlic, finely chopped
2 scotch bonnet or habanero chili peppers, stemmed and finely
    chopped
2 jalapeño chili peppers, stemmed and finely chopped
1 large green bell pepper, stemmed, seeded,
    and cut into small dice
2½ cups coarsely chopped dark chicken meat
2 tablespoons Worcestershire sauce
Salt and pepper, to taste
1 bunch spinach, stemmed and coarsely chopped

Soak the beans overnight in 6 cups of water. Drain well and place in a heavy-bottomed, 6-quart saucepan. Add 8 cups water, chicken stock, allspice, and thyme and bring to a boil over high heat, stirring frequently. Reduce the heat to moderate and cook for 1 hour, stirring occasionally. Add the onion, garlic, chilies, and bell pepper and cook 1 hour, stirring from time to time. Cool slightly.

In a blender, puree the mixture in batches until fairly smooth. Return to the saucepan and bring to a boil over moderate heat. Add the chicken and Worcestershire sauce and cook 15 to 20 minutes, or until the chicken is cooked through. Season with salt and pepper. Stir in the spinach just before serving.

West Indies Chicken Soup with Gouda Cheese

This soul-satisfying soup is made with relatively few ingredients, but the rich, golden squash paired with plump kidney beans, chunks of chicken breast, and nutty Gouda cheese make a premium combination for cool-weather dining.

MAKES ABOUT 9 CUPS.

1 cup dried kidney beans, sorted and washed
16 cups Light Chicken Stock (see page 22)
1 large onion, cut into small dice
1 clove garlic, minced
1 tablespoon ground coriander
1½ teaspoons ground caraway seeds
3 tablespoons olive oil
½ small pumpkin, peeled, seeded, and cut into small dice
(about 2 cups diced squash)
1 cup diced white chicken meat
1 bunch green onions, minced
¾ pound Gouda cheese, grated
Salt and pepper, to taste

Soak the beans in 6 cups of water overnight. Drain well and place in a heavy-bottomed, 6-quart saucepan. Add the chicken stock and bring to a boil over high heat. Reduce the heat to moderate and cook, stirring occasionally, for 2 hours or until the beans are tender.

Using a large saute pan, cook the onion, garlic, and spices in the olive oil over moderate heat for 10 minutes, stirring frequently. Add to the cooked beans and mix well.

Add the pumpkin and bring to a boil over high heat. Cook for 10 minutes, stirring frequently, until the pumpkin is very tender and the mixture is slightly thick. Add the chicken, green onions, and cheese, reduce the heat to moderate, and cook just until the cheese melts and the chicken is cooked through, stirring constantly. Season with salt and pepper and serve immediately.

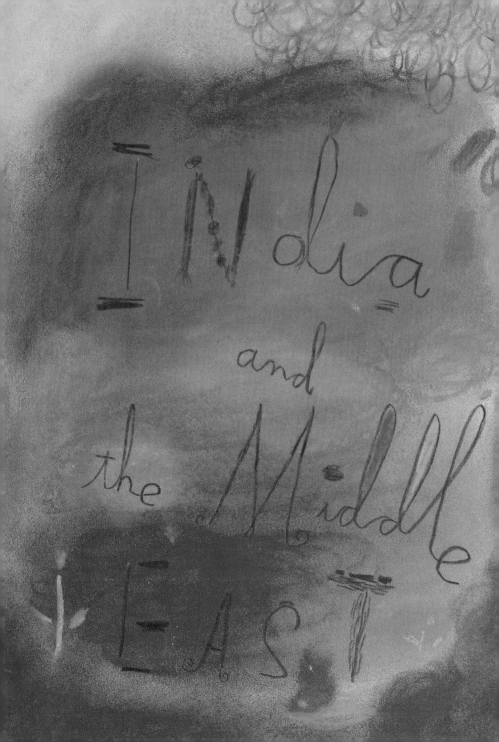

India and the Middle EAST

India and the Middle East

Indian cuisine, known for its fragrant, intoxicating, and intricately combined spice blends, serves as a counterbalance to the more subtly flavored and straightforward Middle Eastern dishes presented in this chapter.

The ingredients, cooking styles, and traditional dishes of India vary greatly from region to region. In general, most East Indian dishes are built on a wide variety of freshly ground spices and herbs combined with fresh vegetables, and, depending on the region and religious practices, lamb, beef, poultry, fish, or seafood. Certain religions forbid the consumption or use of any animal products; for this reason vegetarianism is commonplace in India.

Despite the ever-changing political climate of the Middle East, there remains a strong culinary thread that runs throughout this region. Time-honored classics from countries that technically no longer exist are part of this gustatory heritage, and they live in the hearts and memories of many who originate from these parts. A penchant for combining sweet and sour flavor combinations, along with a passion for garlic and onions, fresh mint and basil, dried beans and rice, and sour cream or yogurt, are evident throughout the recipes from this area.

The soups in this chapter are sophisticated in flavor but for the most part are simple to prepare. In addition, most are quite healthful and nutritious. The inclusion of lentils, cracked wheat, rice, chick-peas, barley, and split peas make many of these soups filling, substantial, and very tasty.

PAstene

170
g. Fancy
TOMATO
PASTE

Moroccan Harira
Chicken SOUP

Moroccan Harira Chicken Soup

Categorized by style rather than region, this North African dish is more typical of Middle Eastern foods—hence its inclusion in this chapter.

Traditionally made with lamb or beef during *Ramadan*—the Muslim month of fasting—this version of *Harira* includes many of the customary herbs and spices, but instead of red meat, I have substituted chicken. With hints of spicy sweetness, this soup is a meal in itself and makes a terrific cold-weather dinner when served with warm bread.

MAKES ABOUT 14 CUPS.

¾ cup dried chick-peas, sorted and washed
2 medium onions, cut into small dice
4 cloves garlic, minced
¼ cup olive oil
2 teaspoons each ground fennel seeds, coriander, and cumin
1 teaspoon ground cinnamon
4 large tomatoes, cored and finely chopped
⅓ cup tomato paste
8 cups Strong Chicken Stock (see page 20)
6 cups water
2 cups finely chopped white chicken meat
6 ounces vermicelli noodles, broken into 1-inch pieces
Salt and pepper, to taste
¾ cup finely chopped fresh parsley, for garnish
¾ cup finely chopped fresh cilantro, for garnish

Soak the chick-peas in 6 cups of water overnight. Drain well and set aside.

In a heavy-bottomed, 6-quart saucepan, cook the onions and garlic in the olive oil over moderate heat for 5 minutes, stirring frequently. Add the spices, tomatoes, and tomato paste and cook over high heat for 5 minutes, stirring constantly. Add the reserved chick-peas, the chicken stock, and 6 cups water and bring to a boil over high heat. Reduce the heat to moderate and cook for 1 hour and 15 minutes, or until the chick-peas are very tender.

Add the chicken and vermicelli noodles and cook for 5 to 7 minutes, stirring frequently, or until the chicken and noodles are tender and just cooked through. Season with salt and pepper. Garnish each portion with parsley and cilantro just before serving.

Indian Chicken Hot-Pot Soup

Called *hotchepot* in some areas, the Indian version of this well-known British stew is made with root vegetables, tomatoes, and sweet and fiery spices. Rather than kidneys and other organ meats and less-than-desirable cuts of inexpensive meat, I have used chicken and chicken stock for this many-layered, complex-tasting soup.

MAKES ABOUT 13 CUPS.

1 large onion, cut into small dice
4 cloves garlic, finely chopped
4 jalapeño chili peppers, stemmed and finely chopped
¼ cup clarified butter or ghee *(recipe follows)*
*1 tablespoon each ground coriander and whole brown
    mustard seeds*
*2 teaspoons each ground fennel seeds, fenugreek, anise seeds,
    cumin, and cayenne pepper*
3-inch piece fresh ginger root, peeled and finely chopped
10 cups Light Chicken Stock (see page 22)
2 cups peeled, seeded, and chopped tomatoes
2 cups chopped, cooked dark chicken meat (see page 13)
1 rutabaga, trimmed, peeled, and cut into medium dice
1 turnip, trimmed, peeled, and cut into medium dice
*1 large carrot, halved lengthwise and cut on the diagonal
    into 1-inch pieces*
1 large boiling potato, cut into medium dice
1 cup fresh or frozen green peas
Salt and pepper, to taste
¾ cup coarsely chopped fresh cilantro, for garnish

In a heavy-bottomed, 6-quart saucepan, cook the onion, garlic, and jalapeño chili peppers in the clarified butter over moderately high heat for 5 minutes, stirring frequently. Add the spices and ginger and cook for 3 to 5 minutes, stirring constantly, until the aroma of spices fills the air. Add the chicken stock, tomatoes, and chicken and bring to a boil over high heat. Reduce the heat to moderate and cook 20 minutes, stirring occasionally.

Add the rutabaga, turnip, carrot, potato, and peas. Cook 15 to 20 minutes or until the vegetables are tender, but not mushy. Season with salt and pepper. Garnish each portion with cilantro just before serving.

To make *ghee:* Place 2 pounds of unsalted butter in a heavy-bottomed saucepan. Cook over moderately low heat for 35 to 40 minutes, stirring frequently, until pale gold and nutty-smelling. Remove from the heat and cool to room temperature.

Carefully pour off the top, upper, clear portion of the liquid, leaving the sediment at the bottom of the pan. Discard the sediment, wipe the pan clean with a paper towel, and return the clear liquid to the pan. Cook over moderately low heat for 10 minutes longer, stirring frequently. Cool to room temperature and strain through several layers of cheesecloth until crystal clear. When cool, pour the strained liquid into a clean jar with a tight-fitting lid, and store in the refrigerator for up to 3 months. Makes approximately 1¾ cups.

Lebanese Chicken and Bulgur Soup

In this Middle Eastern dish cracked wheat provides texture, nutritional value, and a pleasing nutty flavor.

MAKES ABOUT 12 CUPS.

1 large onion, cut into small dice
6 cloves garlic, finely chopped
1 tablespoon ground coriander
2 teaspoons ground cumin
3 tablespoons olive oil
1 cup bulgur (medium-grind cracked wheat)
10 cups Strong Chicken Stock (see page 20)
2 cups chopped dark chicken meat
3 medium tomatoes, cored and cut into small dice
Salt and pepper, to taste
¾ cup coarsely chopped toasted pine nuts, for garnish
1 cup finely chopped fresh parsley, for garnish
¾ cup plain yogurt, for garnish

In a heavy-bottomed, 6-quart saucepan, cook the onion, garlic, and spices in the olive oil over moderate heat for 7 to 10 minutes, stirring frequently. Add the bulgur, chicken stock, and chicken and bring to a boil over high heat. Reduce the heat to moderate and cook for 30 to 35 minutes, stirring occasionally, until the wheat is tender. Add the tomatoes and cook 2 minutes. Season with salt and pepper. Garnish each portion with pine nuts and parsley and drizzle with yogurt just before serving.

Turkish Peasant Soup with Chicken and Barley

Paired with sesame seed crackers or toasted bread and a salad of tender spinach leaves garnished with feta cheese, this nutritious, mild-flavored soup makes a filling cold-weather meal.

MAKES ABOUT 8 CUPS.

1 large onion, cut into small dice
4 cloves garlic, finely chopped
1 tablespoon paprika
2 teaspoons ground cumin
5 tablespoons unsalted butter
¾ cup pearl barley
10 cups Light Chicken Stock (see page 22)
2 cups finely chopped dark chicken meat
2 bell peppers, stemmed, seeded, and finely chopped
Salt and pepper, to taste
1 cup plain yogurt, for garnish
½ cup finely chopped fresh cilantro, for garnish

In a heavy-bottomed, 6-quart saucepan, cook the onion, garlic, and spices in the butter over moderately low heat for 10 minutes, stirring frequently. Add the barley and chicken stock and bring to a boil over high heat. Reduce the heat to moderate and cook for 1 hour, or until the barley is very tender.

Add the chicken and bell peppers and cook for 7 minutes, or until the peppers are tender but not mushy. Season with salt and pepper. Just before serving, garnish each bowl with yogurt and cilantro.

Turkish Chicken and Spinach Soup

This Turkish soup is traditionally made with egg yolks and generous quantities of cream, but the tasty and more healthful version presented here deletes the yolks and is made with a relatively small amount of cream. Easy to make, it takes less than an hour to prepare— even less when using pre-washed, chopped spinach purchased from the grocery store.

MAKES ABOUT 11 CUPS.

4 tablespoons unsalted butter
3 tablespoons all-purpose flour
9 cups Strong Chicken Stock (see page 20)
1 tablespoon each toasted sesame seeds and paprika
2 teaspoons ground cumin
1 cup heavy cream
2 cups finely chopped white chicken meat
Salt and pepper, to taste
1 large bunch spinach, stemmed and julienned
   (about 2 cups)

In a heavy-bottomed, 4-quart saucepan, heat the butter over moderate heat until melted. Add the flour and cook for 5 to 7 minutes, stirring constantly, until the flour is light golden brown and smells nutty.

Slowly add the chicken stock, stirring constantly with a wire whisk to prevent lumps from forming. Add the sesame seeds, paprika, cumin, and cream. Bring to a boil over high heat and cook for 15 minutes, stirring frequently to prevent the mixture from boiling over. Reduce the heat to moderate and cook for 10 minutes, stirring occasionally.

Add the chicken and cook for 5 to 7 minutes, or until the chicken is just cooked through. Season with salt and pepper. Just before serving, add the spinach and mix well.

Persian Chicken and Yellow Split Pea Soup with Mint

This robust soup, spiked with sweet and aromatic spices, is one of my favorites. Its stew-like texture, golden hue, luscious caramelized onion-garlic mixture, and accent of fresh mint and parsley make this an unforgettable Middle Eastern dish.

MAKES ABOUT 14 CUPS.

2 large onions, halved and thinly sliced
7 tablespoons unsalted butter
8 large cloves garlic, finely chopped
1 large bunch green onions, finely chopped
1 tablespoon ground coriander
2 teaspoons each ground cumin and turmeric
1 teaspoon mace
¾ cup dried yellow split peas, sorted and rinsed

½ cup long-grain rice
12 cups Light Chicken Stock (see page 22)
3 large tomatoes, peeled, seeded, and diced
1½ cups finely chopped white chicken meat
⅓ cup fresh lemon juice
Salt and pepper, to taste
¾ cup finely chopped fresh parsley, for garnish
¾ cup finely chopped fresh mint, for garnish

In a large saute pan, cook the onions in 4 tablespoons of the butter over high heat for 5 minutes, stirring frequently. Reduce the heat to low and cook 15 minutes, stirring occasionally, until they are soft and golden brown. Add the garlic and cook 5 to 7 minutes or until the garlic is light golden brown. Remove from the heat and set aside.

In a heavy-bottomed, 6-quart saucepan, cook the green onions and spices in the remaining butter over moderate heat for 3 minutes, stirring frequently. Add the split peas, rice, chicken stock, and tomatoes and bring to a boil over high heat. Reduce the heat to moderate and cook 40 minutes, or until the split peas are tender. Add the chicken and lemon juice and cook 10 minutes, or until the chicken is just cooked through. Season with salt and pepper. Garnish each portion with the reserved onion-garlic mixture, parsley, and mint just before serving.

Mint

12th
century
TEXTILE
WALL
COVERing

Sweet and
Sour Soup

Prunes
ied apples
alnuts
Mint

Persian Sweet-and-Sour Chicken Soup

The ingredients in this Persian soup result in a unique and surprisingly delicious sweet/savory flavor combination.

MAKES ABOUT 14 CUPS.

1 large onion, cut into small dice
4 or 5 tablespoons unsalted butter
1 tablespoon ground coriander
1½ teaspoons each ground cumin, cayenne pepper, and cinnamon
¾ cup long-grain rice
½ cup finely chopped pitted prunes
⅓ cup finely chopped dried apples or pears
11 cups Light Chicken Stock (see page 22)
2 cups finely chopped white chicken meat
½ cup apple cider vinegar or white wine vinegar
½ cup toasted walnuts, finely ground
Salt and pepper, to taste
½ cup finely chopped fresh parsley, for garnish
½ cup finely chopped fresh mint, for garnish (optional)

In a heavy-bottomed, 6-quart saucepan, cook the onion in the butter over moderate heat for 5 minutes, stirring frequently. Add the spices, rice, prunes, apples, and chicken stock. Bring to a boil over high heat. Reduce the heat to moderate and cook for 20 to 25 minutes, stirring occasionally.

Add the chicken, vinegar, and walnuts. Cook for 10 minutes, or until the chicken is just cooked through. Season with salt and pepper. Garnish each portion with parsley and mint just before serving.

The
Mediterranean

THE MEDITERRANEAN

In this chapter we explore the popular cuisines of Greece, Italy, France, Portugal, and Spain. While these countries share many of the same ingredients, divergent combinations of both familiar and unusual foods coupled with distinctive cooking styles produce a wonderfully eclectic collection of recipes.

Sun-drenched produce such as plump tomatoes, glossy eggplant, crisp fresh fennel, asparagus, and zucchini appears in many of these delectable soups. Bright flavors are created in part by tart lemon juice or balsamic vinegar and the generous use of fresh herbs such as basil, rosemary, thyme, marjoram, and sage. More intense tones are introduced through ingredients like oil-cured olives, hard, aged cheeses, and spicy sausages. Many soups from these regions are based on dried beans, rice, or pasta, but some are just straightforward combinations of fresh vegetables, chicken, and stock infused with fresh herbs and olive oil.

As we grow more and more health conscious, foods and recipes from these countries are becoming more popular. The use of olive oil instead of butter or lard in cooking, the abundance of fresh vegetables, and the inclusion of pasta, potatoes, and dried beans favored in these parts make Mediterranean-style cooking a healthful choice. In addition to their nutritious attributes, these soups are worth making for their sunny, delicious flavors.

Greek Avgolemono Soup

I prefer using Meyer lemons in this classic Greek soup, but any variety will do.

MAKES ABOUT 14 CUPS.

1 large onion, cut into small dice
4 cloves garlic, finely chopped
¼ cup olive oil
1½ teaspoons dried thyme
¾ cup long-grain white rice
12 cups Strong Chicken Stock (see page 20)
4 large eggs, lightly beaten
2 cups finely chopped, cooked white chicken meat (see page 13)
½ to ¾ cup fresh lemon juice, to taste
Salt and pepper, to taste
½ cup finely chopped fresh parsley

In a heavy-bottomed, 4-quart saucepan, cook the onion and garlic in the olive oil over moderately low heat for 10 minutes, stirring frequently. Add the thyme and rice and cook 1 minute. Add the chicken stock and bring to a boil over high heat. Reduce the heat to moderate and cook 15 to 20 minutes, or until the rice is tender but not mushy.

Spoon 1½ cups of the hot soup into a large bowl. Slowly add the eggs to the bowl of soup, whisking constantly to prevent the eggs from curdling. Slowly add 1½ additional cups of soup to the egg mixture, whisking constantly. Slowly add the egg-soup mixture to the pot of soup, stirring constantly. Add the chicken, lemon juice, salt, and pepper and mix well. Just before serving, garnish each portion with parsley.

Italian Chicken Broth with Potato Gnocchi

If you have never made these "Italian dumplings," you're in for a treat. I've found that baked rather than boiled potatoes make lighter *gnocchi*. In order to create the lightest, most tender *gnocchi*, work the dough as little as possible and use only enough flour to bind the potatoes.

The broth in this recipe is made from reduced chicken stock, which naturally thickens as it boils. Use only homemade chicken stock for this dish, as canned chicken broth does not thicken as well as homemade stock.

MAKES 10 TO 12 SERVINGS (ABOUT 120 GNOCCHI).

2½ pounds baking potatoes (about 4 large potatoes)
2½ teaspoons salt
1¼ to 1½ cups all-purpose flour
10 cups Strong Chicken Stock (see page 20)
1 tablespoon minced fresh thyme
3 cloves garlic, minced
Salt and pepper, to taste
3 ounces finely grated Parmesan cheese

Preheat oven to 400°F. Bake the potatoes on the middle rack of the oven for 50 to 55 minutes, or until they are tender when pierced with a sharp knife. Remove from the oven and cool to room temperature. Peel the potatoes and discard the skin. Using the finest setting of a cheese grater, grate the potatoes into a medium bowl.

Add the salt and mix gently, using a fork. Add as little flour as possible to form a soft, smooth, consistent mixture. Divide the mixture into eight cylinders. Roll each cylinder into a log approximately 12 to 13 inches long. Cut each log into ¾-inch lengths. Using the sharp tines of a fork, press the tips of the tines onto each *gnocchi*, making an impression of the fork on the surface of the dumpling. This indentation helps the sauce, or in this case, the reduced chicken stock, adhere to the *gnocchi*.

Place the chicken stock, thyme, and garlic in a 6-quart saucepan. Bring to a boil over high heat and cook for 15 minutes, stirring from time to time. Add the *gnocchi* and return to a boil. Cook for 1 to 2 minutes, or until the *gnocchi* float to the surface. Season the soup with additional salt and pepper. Divide the *gnocchi* into separate bowls and cover each with some of the liquid. Serve immediately, garnished with the cheese.

Southern Italian Chicken-chickpea soup with olives

Oil

cured

Olives au citron

Façon Grece

= olives vertes aux piments

rustic robust

Garnish with cheese

Rogers

Southern Italian Chicken-Chick-Pea Soup with Olives

This is one of my favorite soups. Rustic, robust, and earthy, it is most welcome in cold weather and is even better when served with a big, dry red Italian wine, rosemary foccacia, and a salad of mixed mild and bitter greens.

I prefer using home-cooked dried chick-peas in this soup, but canned chick peas can be substituted if you are pressed for time. Add them along with the chicken stock.

MAKES ABOUT 16 CUPS.

2 cups dried chick-peas, washed and sorted
   (about 6 cups cooked chick-peas)
2 bay leaves
1 large onion, cut into small dice
8 cloves garlic, finely chopped
½ cup olive oil
2 large bulbs fennel, trimmed and cut into small dice
1 tablespoon minced fresh thyme, oregano, sage, and rosemary
1 14-ounce can peeled, seeded, and chopped tomatoes
   (about 2 cups)
12 cups Strong Chicken Stock (see page 20)
2 cups chopped dark chicken meat
½ cup finely chopped, pitted, oil-cured olives
Salt and pepper, to taste
2 cups fine bread crumbs
½ cup finely minced fresh parsley
6 ounces finely grated Parmesan cheese, for garnish

Soak the chick-peas in 8 cups of water overnight. Drain well and place in a 6-quart heavy-bottomed saucepan with 12 cups fresh water and the bay leaves. Bring to a boil over high heat. Reduce the heat to moderate and cook for 25 to 30 minutes or until the beans are tender. Drain well and set aside until needed.

In a heavy-bottomed, 6-quart saucepan, cook the onion and garlic in ¼ cup of the olive oil over moderately high heat for 5 minutes, stirring frequently. Add the fennel and herbs and cook for 3 minutes, stirring frequently. Add the tomatoes, chicken stock, chicken, and reserved chick-peas. Bring to a boil over high heat, stirring frequently. Reduce the heat to moderate and simmer for 20 to 25 minutes or until the chick-peas are very tender. Add the olives and season with salt and pepper.

In a large saute pan, heat the remaining olive oil over moderately high heat until it is hot, but not smoking. Add the bread crumbs and cook, stirring constantly, until they are golden brown and their aroma fills the air. Cool to room temperature before adding the parsley; mix well. Spoon the soup into individual bowls and add 2 to 3 tablespoons of the bread crumb mixture to each. Garnish with some of the cheese and serve immediately. Serve the remaining cheese at the table.

Spanish Cream of Chicken Soup with Almonds

Melding a traditional cream of chicken soup with the classic Spanish almond soup called *cebollada con almendras* results in this rich and creamy mixture with pronounced almond overtones.

MAKES ABOUT 6 CUPS.

2 medium onions, coarsely chopped
2 cloves garlic, coarsely chopped
1 bulb fennel, trimmed and coarsely chopped
1 teaspoon dried thyme
¼ cup olive oil
½ cup dry sherry
9 cups Light Chicken Stock (see page 22)
1 cup finely ground almonds
1 cup heavy cream
1½ cups finely chopped, cooked white chicken meat (see page 13)
Salt and pepper, to taste
¼ cup finely chopped fresh parsley, for garnish

In a heavy-bottomed, 4-quart saucepan, cook the onions, garlic, fennel, and thyme in the olive oil over high heat for 5 minutes, sitrring constantly. Add the sherry, reduce the heat to moderate, and cook 5 minutes or until the liquid has evaporated. Add the chicken stock, almonds, and cream and bring to a boil over high heat. Reduce the heat to moderate and cook 25 minutes. Add the chicken and cook 5 minutes, or until the chicken is heated through. Season with salt and pepper. Garnish each portion with parsley just before serving.

Spicy Spanish Chicken and Chorizo Soup

Look for firm, spicy Spanish-style *chorizo* sausage in Latin or Italian grocery stores. Unlike the Mexican variety, Spanish *chorizo* holds its shape when cooked, making it ideal for use in soups. Since most *chorizo* is made with a considerable amount of fat, you may want to skim the surface of this soup prior to serving.

A mixed green salad and a loaf of crusty warm bread served with a saucer of fruity olive oil for dipping would make this a memorable meal.

MAKES ABOUT 14 CUPS.

1 large red onion, cut into medium dice
6 cloves garlic, finely chopped
3 tablespoons olive oil
2 teaspoons each dried oregano, paprika, and cayenne pepper
½ teaspoon ground cinnamon
½ cup dry white wine
1 cup peeled and chopped tomatoes
8 cups Strong Chicken Stock (see page 20)
1 pound spicy Spanish-style chorizo, *each sausage halved and cut into ½-inch-wide half-moons (about 2½ cups sliced sausage)*
2½ cups chopped, cooked dark chicken meat (see page 13)
2 pimentos, or 1 large red bell pepper, stemmed, seeded, and cut into small dice
Salt and pepper, to taste
½ cup chopped fresh parsley, for garnish

In a heavy-bottomed, 6-quart saucepan, cook the onion and garlic in the olive oil over moderate heat for 5 minutes, stirring frequently. Add the herbs, spices, wine, and tomatoes and cook for 10 minutes, stirring frequently.

Add the stock and *chorizo* and bring to a boil over high heat, stirring frequently. Reduce the heat to moderate and cook for 15 minutes, stirring occasionally. Add the chicken and pimento and cook 10 minutes. Season with salt and pepper. Garnish each portion with parsley just before serving.

cup of spicy soup.

Olio extra
Vergine
di
Oliva

Sicilian
chicken
with
asparagus
and
fava
beans

Sicilian Chicken Soup with Asparagus and Fava Beans

This traditional soup cries spring! There's nothing like the texture, color, and flavor of those irresistible, labor-of-love fresh fava beans, which are a staple of Mediterranean cooking. If you cannot find fresh fava beans, substitute cooked baby lima beans and add along with the chicken stock.

MAKES ABOUT 11 CUPS.

2 pounds fresh fava beans, shelled (about 1 cup shelled)
3 large leeks, trimmed, halved, and cut into ½-inch half-moons
    (see page 139)
4 cloves garlic, finely chopped
¼ cup olive oil
10 cups Light Chicken Stock (see page 22)
1 pound asparagus, trimmed and cut into ½-inch pieces
2 cups shredded, cooked dark chicken meat (see page 13)
1½ teaspoons each fresh minced thyme, rosemary, oregano,
    and parsley
Salt and pepper, to taste
Extra-virgin olive oil, for drizzling (optional)

In a medium saucepan, bring 1 quart of salted water to a boil. Add the fava beans and cook 1 minute. Drain in a colander and rinse with cold water. Set aside until cool enough to handle. To remove the fava bean from the pale green outer shell, use your fingernails to "snip" a small opening at the smooth end of the bean, gently push the fava bean from its shell, and place it in a small bowl. Discard the outer shells and set the fava beans aside.

In a heavy-bottomed, 4-quart saucepan, cook the leeks and the garlic in the olive oil over high heat for 5 minutes, stirring frequently. Add the chicken stock and bring to a boil over high heat. Reduce the heat to moderate and cook 20 minutes. Add the asparagus, chicken, herbs, and reserved fava beans, then cook 2 or 3 minutes, or until the asparagus is just tender and bright green. Season with salt and pepper. Drizzle each serving with olive oil, if desired, and serve immediately.

Portuguese Chicken-Kale Soup with Linguiça

Look for *linguiça*, a traditional Portuguese sausage, in upscale grocery stores, Italian markets, or in ethnic butcher shops. If you can't find *linguiça*, use a firm, spicy pork sausage instead.

MAKES ABOUT 14 CUPS.

2 large onions, cut into medium dice
4 cloves garlic, finely chopped
3 tablespoons olive oil
2 linguiça *sausages, cut into ½-inch rounds*
2 teaspoons dried thyme
3 medium white or red boiling potatoes (about 1 pound),
  cut into medium dice
12 cups Strong Chicken Stock (see page 20)
2 cups coarsely chopped, cooked dark chicken meat (see page 13)
1 medium bunch kale, trimmed and coarsely chopped
  (about 4 cups)
Salt and pepper, to taste

In a heavy-bottomed, 6-quart saucepan, cook the onion and garlic in the olive oil over moderate heat for 10 minutes, stirring frequently. Add the sausage and thyme and cook for 2 to 3 minutes, stirring constantly, until the sausage is light golden brown on all sides. Add the potatoes, stock, and chicken and bring to a boil over high heat. Reduce the heat to moderate and cook for 15 to 20 minutes, or until the potatoes are tender. Add the kale and cook for 3 minutes, or just until it wilts. Season with salt and pepper and serve immediately.

Tuscan Chicken Soup with White Beans and Pasta

This comforting Italian stewlike soup is best made with *tubetti* or other small, tube-shaped pasta. If you are pressed for time, feel free to use canned canneloni beans instead of cooking the dried beans, and add them with the chicken stock. Serve with warm bread, Italian cheeses, and a green salad.

MAKES ABOUT 12 CUPS.

*1 cup dried Great Northern white beans, washed
    and sorted (about 3 cups cooked)*
Salt and pepper, to taste
1 large onion, cut into small dice
6 cloves garlic, minced
3 stalks celery, cut into small dice
1 large carrot, cut into small dice
1 tablespoon each dried rosemary, oregano, and thyme
3 tablespoons olive oil
12 cups Strong Chicken Stock (see page 20)
¾ cup tubetti or other small tube-shaped pasta
2 cups chopped, cooked dark chicken meat (see page 13)
2 large zucchini, cut into medium dice
¼ cup extra-virgin olive oil, for drizzling
3 ounces grated imported Parmesan cheese, for garnish

Soak the beans in 6 cups of water overnight. Drain well and place in a saucepan with 6 cups of fresh water. Bring to a boil over high heat. Reduce the heat to moderate and cook for 1 hour to 1 hour and 15 minutes, or until the beans are tender. Drain well, season with salt and pepper, and set aside.

In a heavy-bottomed, 6-quart saucepan, cook the onion, garlic, celery, carrot, and herbs in the olive oil over moderately high heat for 15 minutes, stirring frequently.

Add the chicken stock, pasta, reserved beans, and chicken and bring to a boil over high heat. Reduce the heat to moderate and cook for 10 minutes. Add the zucchini and cook 5 to 7 minutes, stirring occasionally. Adjust the seasoning for salt and pepper. Drizzle each bowl of soup with a little olive oil, garnish with grated cheese, and serve immediately.

oregano

Provençal Chicken

and vegetable soup with Pesto

Rogers

Provençal Chicken and Vegetable Soup with Pesto

Light and healthful, this colorful soup contains some of my favorite vegetables. Fresh baby artichokes are almost always available at my local produce market, but if you can't locate them, or haven't the time to prepare them, use jarred, marinated artichoke hearts instead. Drain before adding to the soup.

MAKES ABOUT 13 CUPS.

3 large leeks, trimmed, halved, and cut into ¼-inch-wide
half-moons (see page 139)
2 cloves garlic, minced
3 tablespoons olive oil
2 teaspoons each minced fresh thyme and oregano
10 cups Light Chicken Stock (see page 22)
18 small baby artichokes, trimmed and halved (about 3 cups)
(see page 140)
1 large red bell pepper, roasted, stemmed, seeded, and cut into
small dice (see page 141)
1 large yellow bell pepper, roasted, stemmed, seeded, and cut
into small dice (see page 141)
3 large tomatoes, cored and cut into small dice
2 cups diced white chicken meat
Salt and pepper, to taste

> *1 large bunch basil, leaves only*
> *3 cloves garlic, chopped*
> *1 ounce Parmesan cheese, grated*
> *¼ cup pine nuts*
> *¾ cup olive oil*
> *Salt and pepper, to taste*

In a heavy-bottomed, 6-quart saucepan, cook the leeks and garlic in the olive oil over moderately high heat for 5 to 7 minutes, stirring frequently. Add the herbs and chicken stock and bring to a boil over high heat. Add the artichokes, bell peppers, tomatoes, and chicken. Reduce the heat to moderate and cook for 10 minutes, stirring occasionally. Season with salt and pepper.

Meanwhile, make the pesto. Place the basil, garlic, cheese, pine nuts, and olive oil in a blender. Puree until smooth and creamy. Season with salt and pepper. Spoon the soup into individual bowls and add 2 to 3 teaspoons of pesto to each just before serving.

Northern Europe, RUSSIA and the Adriatic

Northern Europe, Russia, and the Adriatic

Recipes in this chapter are drawn from the countries of Germany, Hungary, Denmark, Yugoslavia, and the former Soviet Union. To a great extent, culinary practices in these regions are steeped in tradition; many present-day dishes follow virtually the same format and include the same ingredients that are described in original recipes created hundreds of years ago.

The Northern European countries of Germany, Hungary, and Denmark and many districts of Russia depend greatly on such ingredients as butter, cream, and cheese for much of their cooking. These rich ingredients add sustenance and a hefty portion of much-needed calories to help the residents of these areas endure their cold, harsh environments. The availability of fresh produce and spices and fresh herbs has been somewhat limited in many of these countries, yet despite these constraints, a nutritious diet developed.

Potatoes, cabbage, and mushrooms play a large role in the diets of Northern Europeans and Russians, as do cured and salted meats, sausages, and of course, chicken. Yugoslavia, with its expansive coast-line adjacent to the Adriatic Sea, enjoys the luxury of fresh fish and seafood. The classic Russian soups utilize fresh and dried mushrooms, grains and legumes, nuts and seeds, as well as a few fresh vegetables such as onions, garlic, root vegetables, and cabbage.

These recipes are inviting, restorative, and rib-sticking. Most produce filling, substantial soups that are heartier than many in the aforementioned chapters. They are ideal for serving to those who hunger for earthy, comforting meals comprised of a few honest ingredients.

German Chicken and Cabbage Soup with Garlic Sausage

This traditional German soup is spiked with the essence of caraway and celery.

MAKES ABOUT 11 CUPS.

1 large onion, cut into small dice
2 teaspoons ground caraway seeds
1 teaspoon ground celery seeds
2 tablespoons unsalted butter
1 tablespoon olive or vegetable oil
2 large new potatoes (about ¾ pound), cut into small dice
10 cups Light Chicken Stock (see page 22)
¾ pound garlic sausage, cut into ½-inch-thick rounds
2 cups coarsely chopped, cooked dark chicken meat (see page 13)
½ large head white cabbage, cored and finely shredded
  (about 4 cups)
Salt and pepper, to taste
½ cup minced fresh parsley, for garnish

In a heavy-bottomed, 6-quart saucepan, cook the onion and spices in the butter and olive oil over moderate heat for 10 minutes, stirring frequently. Add the potatoes, chicken stock, and sausage and bring to a boil over high heat. Reduce the heat to moderate and cook for 7 to 10 minutes, or until the potatoes are tender. Add the chicken and cabbage and cook for 3 to 5 minutes, or until the cabbage is just wilted. Season with salt and pepper. Garnish each portion with parsley just before serving.

Hungarian Chicken Goulash

This wonderful cold-weather soup would be sensational with a salad made from raw shredded cabbage and finely sliced red onions mixed with a little sour cream. Serve with crackers or bread.

MAKES ABOUT 12 CUPS.

¼ pound bacon
2 medium onions, cut into small dice
2 cloves garlic, finely chopped
1 cup dry white wine
1½ tablespoons paprika
1½ teaspoons caraway seeds
8 cups Light Chicken Stock (see page 22)
2 medium tomatoes, cored and cut into small dice
3 medium boiling potatoes (about 1 pound), cut into small dice
1 cup tiny star-shaped pasta (or other tiny pasta)
2 cups shredded, cooked dark chicken meat (see page 13)
2 medium green bell peppers, stemmed, seeded,
  and cut into small dice
Salt and pepper, to taste

In a heavy-bottomed, 6-quart saucepan, cook the bacon over moderate heat until crisp and golden brown. Remove with a slotted spoon and drain on paper towels. When cool, coarsely chop and set aside. Leave the bacon fat in the pot.

Cook the onion and garlic in the bacon fat over moderate heat for 5 minutes, stirring frequently. Add the white wine, paprika, and caraway seeds and cook 10 minutes, or until the liquid evaporates.

Add the chicken stock and tomatoes, bring to a boil over high heat, and cook for 5 minutes, stirring frequently. Add the potatoes, pasta, chicken, green peppers, and reserved bacon. Reduce the heat to moderate and cook for 15 minutes, stirring from time to time, until the potatoes are tender. Season with salt and pepper.

potato

caraway

garlic

parsley

dill

German Potato-Leek Soup with Chicken

In this soul-satisfying soup, potatoes are cooked in chicken stock and then pureed, resulting in a smooth, creamy base for sauteed leeks and tender white chicken. For a really low-fat dish, use a nonstick saute pan and cook the leeks and garlic over low heat using one tablespoon of olive oil instead of the butter. You won't enjoy the luscious undertone and richness of the sweet butter, but you may feel better about eating bowl after bowl of this tasty soup.

MAKES ABOUT 12 CUPS.

3 medium boiling potatoes (about 1 pound), peeled and
  cut into eighths
10 cups Strong Chicken Stock (see page 20)
1 teaspoon caraway seeds
3 large leeks, trimmed, halved, and cut into ¼-inch-wide
  half-moons (see page 139)
2 cloves garlic, finely chopped
4 tablespoons unsalted butter
2 cups finely chopped, cooked white chicken meat (see page 13)
Salt and pepper, to taste
¼ cup minced fresh parsley or dill, for garnish

Place the potatoes, 6 cups of the stock, and the caraway seeds in a heavy-bottomed, 6-quart saucepan. Bring to a boil over high heat. Reduce the heat to moderate and cook 25 to 30 minutes, or until the potatoes are very tender. Cool slightly. Using a blender, puree in batches until smooth. Return to the saucepan and set aside.

In a very large saute pan, cook the leeks and garlic in the butter over high heat for 5 to 7 minutes, stirring frequently, until any liquid has evaporated and the leeks are beginning to turn light golden brown.

Add the leeks and the remaining 4 cups chicken stock to the pureed potato mixture. Bring to a boil over high heat. Reduce the heat to moderate and cook for 15 to 20 minutes, stirring occasionally. Add the chicken and cook for 5 minutes, or until the chicken is heated through. Season with salt and pepper. Garnish each portion with parsley or dill just before serving.

Danish Cream of Chicken and Mushroom Soup

This sumptuous soup makes a complete meal when paired with a mixed green salad and a loaf of warm bread.

MAKES ABOUT 8 CUPS.

3 tablespoons olive oil
2 pounds fresh button mushrooms cut into thick slices
2 large leeks, trimmed, and cut into half-moons (see page 139)
2 stalks celery, cut into small dice
1 teaspoon each ground celery seeds and dill seeds
3 tablespoons unsalted butter
6½ cups Light Chicken Stock (see page 22)
2 cups heavy cream
2 cups finely chopped white chicken meat
Salt and pepper, to taste
¼ cup finely chopped fresh parsley, for garnish

In a large, nonstick saute pan, heat 1½ tablespoons of the olive oil over high heat until hot, but not smoking. Add half of the mushrooms and cook over high heat for 5 to 7 minutes, stirring constantly, until the mushrooms are golden brown and any liquid has evaporated. Remove to a bowl and set aside. Cook the second batch of mushrooms in the remaining olive oil in the same manner, and add to the other mushrooms.

In a heavy-bottomed, 6-quart saucepan, cook the leeks, celery, and spices in the butter over moderately high heat for 5 to 7 minutes, stirring frequently, until the leeks and celery are tender. Add the chicken stock, cream, and reserved mushrooms and bring to a boil over high heat. Cook for 15 minutes, stirring frequently to prevent the mixture from boiling over. Add the chicken and reduce the heat to moderate. Cook for 7 to 10 minutes, stirring occasionally, or until the chicken is just cooked through. Season with salt and pepper. Garnish each portion with parsley just before serving.

Hungarian Chicken Soup with Dumplings

Dumplings, traditionally made from a mixture of flour, eggs, butter, milk, and in some cases, chicken liver or cheese, are a fundamental part of Hungarian cooking. The following basic recipe yields just enough tiny, delicate dumplings to add body, texture, and substance to this colorful soup.

MAKES ABOUT 11 CUPS.

DUMPLINGS:

1½ cups all-purpose flour

¾ teaspoon kosher or sea salt

Pepper, to taste

1 large egg, lightly beaten

1½ tablespoons unsalted butter, melted and cooled

¼ cup whole milk

SOUP:

1 medium onion, cut into medium dice

1 large leek, trimmed, halved, and cut into ½-inch-wide half-moons (see page 139)

1½ teaspoons caraway seeds

3 tablespoons unsalted butter or chicken fat

11 cups Strong Chicken Stock (see page 20)

1 parsnip, cut into small dice

1 large carrot, cut into small dice

2 stalks celery, cut into medium dice

2 cups finely chopped dark chicken meat

4 ounces vermicelli noodles, broken into 1-inch lengths

Salt and pepper, to taste

½ cup coarsely chopped fresh parsley, for garnish

To make the dumplings: In a small bowl, combine the flour, salt, pepper, egg, melted butter, and milk. Mix vigorously for 3 or 4 minutes or until the dough holds together and has a smooth texture. If the dough is too wet, add a little more flour; if the dough is too dry, add a little more milk. Turn the dough out onto a lightly floured surface and knead for 1 minute, or until the dough is smooth. Cover with a damp towel or plastic wrap and let stand for 30 minutes. Using a dull knife, cut the dough into small pieces approximately ½ inch long by ¼ inch wide. Set aside until needed.

To make the soup: In a heavy-bottomed, 6-quart saucepan, cook the onion, leek, and caraway seeds in the butter over high heat for 5 minutes, stirring frequently. Add the chicken stock and bring to a boil over high heat. Add the parsnip, carrot, celery, and chicken and return to the boil. Reduce the heat to moderate and simmer for 20 minutes, or until all the vegetables are tender and the chicken is thoroughly cooked.

Add the vermicelli noodles and the dumplings; cook 3 or 4 minutes, or until the dumplings rise to the surface and are thoroughly cooked and the noodles are tender. Season the soup with salt and pepper. Garnish each portion with parsley just before serving.

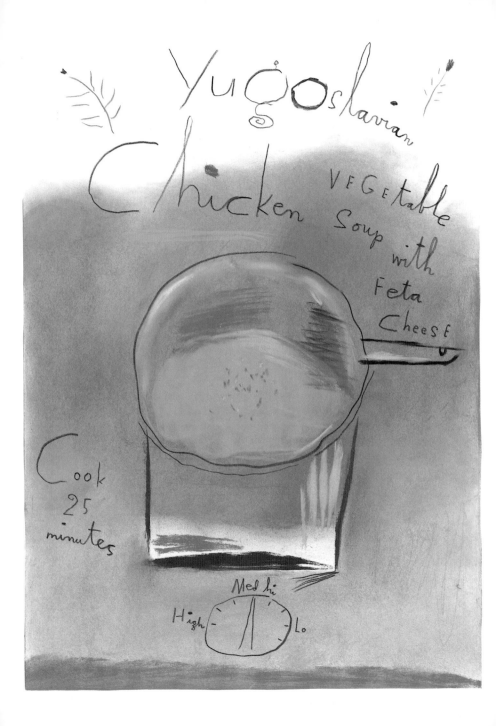

Yugoslavian

Chicken

VEGEtable
Soup with
Feta
Cheese

Cook
25
minutes

Med hi

High   Lo

Yugoslavian Chicken-Vegetable Soup
with Feta Cheese

Velvety chunks of eggplant paired with the familiar flavors of green bell peppers and rice make this soup both comforting and filling. The inclusion of Bulgarian feta cheese adds a tangy flavor and rich texture.

MAKES ABOUT 14 CUPS.

2 medium onions, cut into medium dice

3 cloves garlic, finely chopped

3 tablespoons olive oil or chicken fat

1 cup long-grain white rice

2 teaspoons paprika

2 Italian, Japanese, or Chinese eggplants,
*   cut into medium dice (about 4 cups diced)*

2 cups coarsely chopped tomatoes

12 cups Light Chicken Stock (see page 22)

1 large green bell pepper, stemmed, seeded,
*   and cut into medium dice*

2 cups coarsely chopped dark chicken meat

Salt and pepper, to taste

¾ cup finely chopped fresh parsley, for garnish

¾ pound feta cheese, crumbled

In a heavy-bottomed, 6-quart saucepan, cook the onions and garlic in the olive oil over moderate heat for 10 minutes, stirring frequently. Add the rice, paprika, eggplants, and tomatoes and cook 5 minutes, stirring frequently.

Add the chicken stock, green pepper, and chicken and bring to a boil over high heat. Reduce the heat to moderate and cook 25 minutes, or until the vegetables and rice are tender and the chicken is thoroughly cooked. Season with salt and pepper. Garnish each bowl with parsley and feta cheese just before serving.

Armenian Chicken and Lentil Soup with Dried Apricots

The subtle, sweet undertone of apricots and a rich, golden hue make this soup intriguing. Serve with traditional Armenian flatbread.

MAKES ABOUT 10 CUPS.

1 large onion, cut into small dice
3 cloves garlic, finely chopped
1½ tablespoons white sesame seeds
2 teaspoons each ground coriander, cumin, and paprika
1 teaspoon each ground mace and cayenne pepper
3 tablespoons olive oil or chicken fat
1 cup dried red lentils, sorted and washed
12 cups Strong Chicken Stock (see page 20)
½ cup minced dried apricots
2 cups shredded, cooked dark chicken meat (see page 13)
½ cup fresh lemon juice
Salt and pepper, to taste

In a heavy-bottomed, 6-quart saucepan, cook the onion, garlic, sesame seeds, and spices in the olive oil over moderate heat for 5 to 7 minutes, stirring frequently. Add the lentils, chicken stock, and apricots and bring to a boil over high heat. Reduce the heat to moderate and cook 40 to 50 minutes, or until the lentils are very tender. Add the chicken and lemon juice and cook 5 minutes. Season with salt and pepper.

chantarelle
porcini
PORtabella
mushrooms
гриБы
БЕлыЕ
Rogers

Russian Wild Mushroom-Chicken Soup with Barley and Cheese

If you can't find any of the fresh wild or cultivated varieties mentioned, make the soup with 2½ pounds of button mushrooms instead—the soup won't be as full-flavored and distinctive, but it will still be worth making.

MAKES ABOUT 14 CUPS.

1½ ounces dried porcini mushrooms

5 tablespoons olive oil

*1 pound fresh button mushrooms, halved (if large)
    and sliced into ¼-inch-wide pieces*

*¼ pound each fresh chanterelle, shiitake, portabello, and
    porcini mushrooms, brushed clean, stemmed, and sliced
    into ¼-inch-wide pieces*

1 large onion, cut into small dice

4 tablespoons unsalted butter

2 teaspoons dried thyme

1 teaspoon ground caraway seeds

12 cups Light Chicken Stock (see page 22)

¾ cup pearl barley

1½ cups shredded, cooked dark chicken meat (see page 13)

¼ cup red wine vinegar or balsamic vinegar

Salt and pepper, to taste

¾ pound farmer's or mild-tasting Feta cheese

½ cup finely chopped fresh parsley, for garnish

Soak the porcini mushrooms in 2 cups of boiling water for 30 minutes, or until they are soft and pliable. Remove the mushrooms from the water (reserving the soaking liquid), and using your fingers, remove any sand, grit, or dirt from the mushrooms. Rinse under cold water. Finely chop the mushrooms and set aside. Strain the reserved soaking liquid through several layers of cheesecloth until no grit or dirt remains. Set aside.

In a large, nonstick saute pan, heat 3 tablespoons of the olive oil over high heat until hot, but not smoking. Add the button mushrooms and cook over high heat for 5 to 7 minutes, stirring constantly, until they are golden brown and any liquid has evaporated. Place in a large bowl. In the same pan, heat the remaining olive oil over moderate heat. Add the fresh chanterelle, shiitake, portabello, and porcini mushrooms and cook over a moderate heat 5 to 7 minutes, stirring frequently, until the mushrooms are just tender. Add to the button mushrooms, along with the reserved porcini mushrooms and their soaking liquid. Mix well and season with salt and pepper.

In a heavy-bottomed, 6-quart saucepan, cook the onion in the butter over moderately low heat for 5 minutes, stirring frequently. Add the thyme, caraway seeds, chicken stock, barley, and mushroom mixture and bring to a boil over high heat. Reduce the heat to moderate and cook 40 minutes, stirring occasionally, until the barley is very tender. Add the chicken and vinegar and cook 5 minutes. Season with salt and pepper.

Before serving, add a few teaspoons of cheese and a sprinkling of parsley to each bowl.

Georgian Chicken-Walnut Soup with Red Beans

Plump, red kidney beans and walnuts—two favored ingredients of Georgian cuisine—team up to create a substantial, robust soup ideal for cold winter nights.

MAKES ABOUT 12 CUPS.

1 cup dried kidney beans, sorted and washed
1 large onion, cut into small dice
4 cloves garlic, finely chopped
2 stalks celery, cut into small dice
¼ cup olive oil
2 teaspoons each ground coriander and fenugreek
¾ cup dry white wine
11 cups Strong Chicken Stock (see page 20)
2 cups finely chopped dark chicken meat
¾ cup finely chopped toasted walnuts
¼ cup apple cider or white wine vinegar
Salt and pepper, to taste
½ cup finely chopped fresh cilantro, for garnish

Soak the kidney beans in 8 cups of water overnight. Drain well. Place the beans in a large pot and add 10 cups of cold water. Bring to a boil over high heat, stirring frequently. Reduce the heat to moderate and cook for 1 hour and 20 minutes, or until the beans are tender. Drain well and set aside.

In a heavy-bottomed, 6-quart saucepan, cook the onion, garlic, and celery in the olive oil over moderate heat for 5 minutes, stirring frequently. Add the spices and wine and cook for 5 minutes, or until all the liquid has evaporated. Add the chicken stock, chicken, and reserved beans and bring to a boil over high heat. Reduce the heat to moderate and cook for 30 minutes, stirring occasionally. Add the walnuts and vinegar and cook for 3 minutes. Season with salt and pepper. Garnish each portion with cilantro just before serving.

Notes on Ingredients

Following are a few basic techniques required for preparing and cooking some of the ingredients called for in the following recipes. You may want to take a few minutes to look over these directions for preparing various types of produce; perhaps you will discover an easier way to wash leeks, roast peppers, and prepare fresh baby artichoke hearts.

Hopefully this section will answer most of your questions pertaining to recipes in this book. For more detailed cooking techniques, consult the *Joy of Cooking*, or your favorite resource for this kind of fundamental information.

To Wash and Prepare Leeks: Trim the leeks by cutting across the grain approximately 1 inch beyond the point where the leaves begin to turn dark green. Discard the green leaves, or wash and save to use in stock. Remove two or three outer layers of the tough, fibrous leaves and discard, or wash and save to use in stock.

To make half-moon shapes: Halve the leeks lengthwise. Place the cut side down on a cutting board, and cut across the grain, making half moons the desired width. To make circles, leave the leeks whole and cut across the grain the desired width.

Fill the kitchen sink or a large bowl with cold water. Add the sliced leeks and swish around in the water, separating the layers and removing any dirt, grit, or sand with your fingers. Using your hands, remove the leeks from the water—*do not dump the water out with the leeks*, or all the dirt will fall back onto the vegetables. Drain the leeks in a colander. Discard the dirty water and refill with cold water. Wash the leeks once more using the same technique; drain well in a colander. The leeks are now ready to cook.

To Prepare Fresh Baby Artichoke Hearts:

Using a very sharp knife or cleaver, cut approximately ½ inch off the pointed tip of each choke; discard the tip. Cut away the long stem (if the stem is still attached), and discard. Using your hands, remove the tough, dark green outer leaves from the exterior of the artichoke, stopping when you come to the tender, yellow inner leaves. Using a paring knife, trim the bottom end of each heart, removing any dark, rough, or dry areas, and shaping the end so that it is round and smooth. Cut the artichokes in half from top to bottom if the recipe calls for halved artichoke hearts.

To prevent the trimmed chokes from turning brown while you work, submerge the sliced artichoke hearts in a bowl filled with 3 cups of water mixed with ½ cup lemon juice or white wine vinegar. Drain well before cooking.

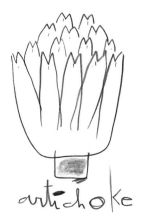

artichoke

To Roast Chili and Bell Peppers: Using a pair of tongs or a long kitchen fork, hold the chili pepper over a gas flame, rotating it until the skin is thoroughly blackened. Place in a plastic bag and seal tightly for 10 to 15 minutes. Remove from the bag and rinse under cool water, removing the blackened skin. (You may want to use rubber gloves when working with hot chili peppers. If you do not wear gloves, avoid touching sensitive skin areas and mucus membranes after handling.)

You can also roast chilies over an open flame on an outdoor barbecue. Simply place the chilies on the rack set over moderately hot or low coals, rotating as the skin blackens. When all sides are black, remove from the heat and follow the aforementioned directions.

To Grind Whole Spices: Use an electric spice or coffee grinder to pulverize whole spices.

ground
Coriander
cumin
cAyenne
tumeric

INDEX

Table of Equivalents

The exact equivalents in the following tables have been rounded for convenience.

US / UK

oz – ounce

lb – pound

in – inch

ft – foot

tbl – tablespoon

fl oz – fluid ounce

qt – quart

LIQUIDS

US	Metric	UK
2 tbl	30 ml	1 fl oz
1/4 cup	60 ml	2 fl oz
1/3 cup	80 ml	3 fl oz
1/2 cup	125 ml	4 fl oz
2/3 cup	160 ml	5 fl oz
3/4 cup	180 ml	6 fl oz
1 cup	250 ml	8 fl oz
1 1/2 cups	375 ml	12 fl oz
2 cups	500 ml	16 fl oz
4 cups/1 qt	1 l	32 fl oz

METRIC

g – gram

kg – kilogram

mm – millimeter

cm – centimeter

ml – milliliter

l – liter

OVEN TEMPERATURES

Fahrenheit	Celsius	Gas
250	120	1/2
275	140	1
300	150	2
325	160	3
350	180	4
375	190	5
400	200	6
425	220	7
450	230	8
475	240	9
500	260	10

WEIGHTS

US/UK	Metric
1 oz	30 g
2 oz	60 g
3 oz	90 g
4 oz (1/4 lb)	125 g
5 oz (1/3 lb)	155 g
6 oz	185 g
7 oz	220 g
8 oz (1/2 lb)	250 g

LENGTH MEASURES

1/8 in	3 mm
1/4 in	6 mm
1/2 in	12 mm
1 in	2.5 cm
2 in	5 cm
3 in	7.5 cm
4 in	10 cm
5 in	13 cm
6 in	15 cm